Collaborative Learning Communities in Middle School Literacy Education

Offering research on afterschool literacy programs designed around teacher-student collaborative inquiry groups, this book demonstrates how adolescent learning is uniquely successful when grounded in dialogic conversation. By providing a robust theoretical framework for this approach in the middle school, Malavasic showcases how developing a learning community which focuses on mutual respect and attention to students' personal academic literacy histories can become the catalyst for the overall success of teaching and learning in the classroom.

Centered on building quality teacher-student relationships and creating a classroom learning community, this book highlights essential topics such as:

- The impact of talk-based critical thinking
- The augmentation on students' motivation, engagement, and identity construction
- Research, theory, and pedagogy
- Celebrating literacy learning

Collaborative Learning Communities in Middle School Literacy Education is the perfect addition for researchers, academics, and postgraduate students in the fields of literacy and those on Teacher Education programs. This volume positions collaborative inquiry learning as an effective way forward for teaching and learning in the middle school and is essential for those wanting to explore this further.

Jolene T. Malavasic is a faculty member in the Department of Literacy Teaching and Learning at the University at Albany. She received her PhD in Reading from Syracuse University. Jolene previously worked as an Assistant Professor in the Literacy Department at SUNY Cortland and as a middle school reading specialist. Her current research explores how teacher-student relationships in collaborative teaching spaces shape and are shaped by adolescents' literate identities and literacy practices in and outside of school.

Collaborative Learning Communities in Middle School Literacy Education

Increasing Student Engagement with Authentic Literacy

Jolene T. Malavasic

Routledge
Taylor & Francis Group

LONDON AND NEW YORK

First published 2020
by Routledge
2 Park Square, Milton Park, Abingdon, Oxon OX14 4RN
605 Third Avenue, New York, NY 10017

First issued in paperback 2020

*Routledge is an imprint of the Taylor & Francis Group, an
informa business*

Library of Congress Cataloging-in-Publication Data
A catalog record for this title has been requested

ISBN 13: 978-0-367-72715-4 (pbk)
ISBN 13: 978-1-138-35397-8 (hbk)

Typeset in Times New Roman
by codeMantra

To my mom, Shirley, thank you for your patience, friendship, and never allowing me to give up on my dreams.

Contents

Figures

Acknowledgments

I approach my journey writing this book from two lenses. First, that of a middle school literacy specialist who spent fifteen years teaching, building relationships, and sharing learning experiences with adolescents, to my current role as a teacher educator in a university setting where I continue to place an emphasis on building relationships and sharing learning experiences as I prepare graduate teachers to be literacy specialists and coaches. In both roles, I have always maintained the lens of a reflective practitioner in that I am cognizant about the connections and implications of my instructional decisions to my teaching practice.

This book would not have been possible without the opportunities I have gained from my experiences in school partnerships. I wish to extend a heartfelt thank you to all the administrators, teachers, and middle school students I have worked with over the past few years. I continue to be grateful for the opportunity to work alongside you. Special thanks to Dr. Sherry Guice for your generosity in allowing us to occupy your classroom space and your supportive efforts to implement this program at Lake Middle School.

A special thank you to all the amazing graduate students who co-teach with me for your insights and contributions to this project. I have learned much from all of you in the process. You continue to inspire me and affirm my love of teaching and learning.

I could not have completed this book without the support and guidance from my mentors, colleagues, and friends, Kathy Hinchman, Carol Santa, Kelly Chandler-Olcott, Donna Mahar, Margi Sheehy, Stephanie Affinito, Stasia Bembenek Bailey, Lana Wagner, and Zach Rossetti. Thanks to all of you for sharing your knowledge, time, and encouraging me along the way.

Finally, I extend many thanks to all who choose to read this book. I hope you will find the contents relevant and valuable to your own work as teachers and researchers.

1 Relationships and Classroom Communities

Why Relationships Matter

As human beings, it is our nature to seek and develop relationships with others. The meanings we attach to our relationships, the expectations we hold for them, and the value we give to them are largely dependent upon the context in which they take place. Sometimes these relationships serve as the groundwork for change. When thinking about the contexts of relationships in schools, we can draw upon these same notions. Santa (2006) articulated it best when she described schools and classrooms as communities and microcosms of the larger society. If students feel disconnected in school, they will often disengage which can lead them to not be successful. Yet, fostering relationships with our students is not just about getting them to like us. In some instances, creating relationships with students can be more significant than the content we teach. Consider the way students, in particular, adolescents, navigate the multiple relationships in their lives, and where the social organization and culture of the classroom not only influence learning practices, but those same learning practices also shape the social organization and cultural patterns that develop in the classroom (Wells, 1996).

More often than not, students achieve better in classrooms when there is a sense of community where classroom members feel comfortable interacting with each other and the teacher (Wolk, 2003). Lee, Smith, Perry, and Smylie's (1999) research aligns with this notion. They observed teachers' interactions and relationships with their sixth- and eighth-grade students in the Chicago Schools, using an approach called "social support" that focused on strengthening relationships among teachers and students in and outside of school. They examined the levels of social support among teachers and students in four areas and noted to what degree did teachers know their students, listen to what their students said, relate the subject they taught to students' personal interests, and hold the belief their students could do well in school. Their findings should not be surprising. Clearly, those classrooms where social support levels were high achieved the highest gains on standardized math and reading tests, thus reaffirming the need for quality relationships.

We should not jump to conclude that the ultimate goal of the above factors along with supportive, caring relationships among teachers and students should only be outcomes on test scores. Rather, we should be looking at how we can cultivate students' success not just as test takers, but also thinkers, learners, and as people who will make valuable contributions to our future society. Work by Daniels and Zemelman (2014) reminds us that although there are multiple ways for teachers to build supportive relationships with their students, we should also consider trust as a fundamental factor to their success. This is where we again look to the classroom itself as a place to build a trusting community where students' voices are heard and validated, and there are opportunities for students to be responsible classroom participants in an environment that is safe and encourages them to take risks.

I have always believed that educators have a keen interest in developing supportive relationships with students and colleagues, but sometimes these are seen as rushed "add ons" or supplements to instruction rather than devoting time to see them as a potential to become an essential part within the instruction itself. In my experiences as a middle school reading specialist and teacher educator, I have found time to be one of the key factors contributing to the overall effectiveness of relationship-building. Taking time to build quality relationships are at the core of successful learning outcomes for teachers and students. Yet, we can't assume this will happen immediately; rather, it has to be an ongoing process, especially when teachers do not yet have background teaching in their own classrooms. In my experiences as a teacher educator, I discovered that most of my graduate students do not have extensive knowledge or practice engaging in supportive relationships with students, either as students themselves or in their prior teacher preparation. It was important to devote time in this course supporting the knowledge acquisition of developing teachers to broaden their understandings of why teacher-student relationships and engaging curriculum are equally important and using the design of the course to show how they can be interwoven thorough collaborative inquiry groups. Combining the first two factors with practical experiences in collaborative contexts allows teachers new to the field time to acquire and refine the tools they need to create these environments independently.

As the instructor of the course, I knew it was essential to embed time for the graduate teachers to learn how to form quality relationships with the middle school students in their collaborative teaching groups, and collegial professional learning communities with each other through their teaching partnerships and daily seminar sessions. These will become central to their future positions as literacy specialists working with students, teachers, families, and communities, and as literacy coaches working with similar stakeholders in the school community and professional development beyond the school setting.

The design of this book centers on two essential keys to successful learning experiences for adolescents: building relationships and creating a collaborative learning community. It details how collective knowledge building through student-teacher collaborative learning communities provides opportunities for teachers to experience the unique and personal academic literacy histories adolescent students possess that influence who they choose to develop relationships with, how they value literacy, and shape how they view their work. The interactions within these learning communities play a significant role in mediating multiple modes of being a reader and writer for the middle school participants. In the dialogical discussions among the collaborative inquiry groups, middle school students engage with multiple texts to express their opinions, emotions, and design multimodal texts that connect to their personal literate lives.

My primary intent in writing this book is to inform researchers, teacher educators preparing secondary undergraduate and graduate students, and teachers who interact with adolescents of the ongoing opportunity to revise and expand what we know about adolescents' lives, relationships, and literacy practices. In the coming pages, my goal is to provide those affiliated with secondary education ways to create spaces for success within which students have multiple opportunities to enhance their competencies, rather than limiting to confining spaces that label and restrict such displays and growth. As Hull and Schultz (2001) suggested, there continue to be vast gulfs that have widened between students who flourish in school and those that do not. Such division can be especially seen between the privileged and disenfranchised students who have limited opportunities based on the out-of-school resources available to them. It makes sense, then, for educators to look for ways to consider relationships among students' personal and transformed literacy practices in their efforts to increase the learning and success of all students.

Students come to school with a myriad of experiences to make sense of the new knowledge they learn or continue to learn, and they utilize their school knowledge in their lives outside of school. Rather than knowing students by their competencies displayed only on standardized tests, teachers who acknowledge the potential of relationships and multiliteracies of their students might come to a better understanding of the lives their students describe. Although what I note above is applicable to all students, it is of particular relevance to adolescents.

Connections among Relationships, Communities, and Collaborative Teaching

The course described in this book is structured around three central components: building relationships through collaborative grouping, fostering student achievement using literacy events, and designing curriculum via knowledge units to teach argumentative reading and writing. It is a required course for graduate students seeking to become secondary literacy specialists and coaches as there is a practicum component for those seeking either B-12 or 5–12 certification. This is considered a capstone experience where graduate students are required to complete twenty-five practicum hours working with middle school students. The course meets twice a week for three hours in an afterschool setting.

The purpose for offering the course afterschool is twofold: first, to accommodate graduate students, many of whom are full-time teachers; second, to provide a unique opportunity for middle school students to experience collaborative learning with a range of literacy events and knowledge building that extends beyond the school context and is designed to further bridge the in-school and out-of-school literacies of the middle school students. As Alvermann (2009) noted, it is important that teachers create opportunities where students can actively engage in meaningful subject matter learning that encompasses and expands on the literacy practices they already possess and value.

Forming School Partnerships

In the newly released International Literacy Association Standards for the Preparation of Literacy Professionals (2018) Standard 7.3 under Practicum/Clinical Experiences recommends that "candidates have ongoing opportunities for authentic, school-based practicum experiences" (p. 3). In order to support this suggestion, an essential part of our work in teacher preparation involves building partnerships with schools. In my experiences as a reading specialist and teacher educator, I have been involved in multiple practicum partnerships.

As a teacher educator seeking to build a school partnership, I have found the most difficult challenge, but one that I readily embrace, is getting "off the ground" by requesting and securing a location. When forming the initial school partnership for the collaborative inquiry course, I communicated via email with a reading specialist at an area middle school with whom I had developed a prior professional relationship. She and I set up a time to meet at her school the semester prior to the scheduled class. At the meeting, I presented her the framework of the course, and we discussed how it would fit into the context of the school community and the middle school students. She was immediately enthusiastic about the idea and the opportunity it provided students. She made arrangements for us to meet and discuss the course further with the school principal and English-Language Arts teacher who were eager about forming the partnership. The principal made a recommendation to the school superintendent who negotiated all the remaining logistical details with our department and the university.

There were some final logistical steps to complete a few weeks prior the start of the semester. They included securing classroom space at the school, going over the days and dates that needed to be allocated for student participation, and further detailing the components of the program with the teachers involved so they could promote the class to enlist student participants. In addition to the teachers' assistance, I created a letter that was sent electronically to all families via an email from the school. The letter contained preliminary information about the structure and content of the course along with an invitation for students to participate. I should note there were no limitations, requirements, or incentives regarding student participants (Figure 1.1).

Dear Families,

For the third year as a part of our Secondary Literacy Masters' program we are excited to extend an opportunity for your child to participate in our *Reading and Writing Inquiry Groups* to be held at your school. The program will meet Tuesdays and Thursdays from 4-5:30pm. Our first day will be Thursday February 7th, and our last day concludes with our family celebration on Thursday, May 2nd. During this time your child will be working collaboratively in small groups consisting of two to three middle school students and two graduate students. The groups will be exploring argumentative writing and multiple literacies through the reading of a variety of texts, using various digital media, discussions, and exploring different genres of writing. As always, we look forward to working with students at Lake School, and I hope that your child will be able to participate. **Please do not hesitate to contact me or your child's teacher should you have any questions.**

Sincerely,
Dr. Jolene T. Malavasic

Figure 1.1 Sample invitation letter to families.

The letter is an invitation welcoming any students who have an interest in participating. I generally have a warm response to the letter and always have a generous number of students who want to participate. When I receive the names of those interested participants, I always reach out with further correspondence either via email or a phone call. I feel it is important to foster a relationship with families early to let them know how much we appreciate the opportunity to work with their child since they too are making an investment in the class. As a matter of fact, I now have students returning to participate for another year and siblings of some of the former student participants involved in the collaborative group practicum because they [prior students] spoke so highly of their experience. As you will read in the concluding chapter, I regularly receive compliments either in person, via emails, and written notes from the middle school student participants, their families, the school community, and positive comments from the graduate teacher participants in the course.

As I will discuss further in the next chapter, before our first meeting day with the middle school students, the graduate teachers and I spend four-five class days reading and discussing literature about many topics, including adolescence and adolescents, identity, classroom learning communities, etc., to name a few. During this time, graduate teachers work with their colleagues to build relationships and establish their own professional learning communities. They do this by creating and sharing identity webs, engaging in dialogical discussion and developing the instructional components of the knowledge units, and designing the unit presentations they will share on day one with the middle school students.

Although the context for this book expands upon the above work in an afterschool partnership between a middle school and university, I believe it can easily be adapted to multiple contexts. I believe this book further broadens the impact of learning communities for adolescent students. It validates, with supportive evidence, why successful teaching outcomes are often the result of supportive student-teacher relationships that enable teachers to weave various experiences and provide opportunities for students to develop as sophisticated readers and writers (Serafini 2001).

As you will read about in the coming chapters, the middle school student participants developed a sense of efficacy, shifts in their knowledge of the multiple literacy events around argumentative reading and writing, and confidence in ways of learning as a result of their connections with teachers and the collaborative environment created within the inquiry groups. My hope is the range of readers of this text will envision how they can apply this innovative framework to their own pedagogical practices.

Within the subsequent chapters, I lay out a theoretical foundation behind the program design, detail the two elements of the course, practicum and seminar, explain the essential components of the practicum such as construction of the knowledge units, multimodal texts used, descriptions of the five literacy events guided reading, discussion, word work, and writing workshop that were a part of each unit cycle, and provide insights into how middle school students designed their multimodal culminating projects. There will be vignettes that portray how the relationships, collaborative literacy practices, instructional strategies and activities within the learning communities weaved together to become integral components to the overall successful outcomes for students and teachers.

2 Research, Theory, and Pedagogy

Course Development

The background surrounding the design of this course is deeply rooted in ongoing discussions in the literacy field around content area and disciplinary literacy and the impact it has had on our teacher preparation programs, particularly at the secondary level. First, I want to focus the discussion on the foundation behind this course and how it became part of a two-course sequence I designed with my colleague, Margi Sheehy.

We teach in a graduate program preparing masters students for secondary literacy specialization to be secondary literacy specialists and coaches. An ongoing teacher preparation challenge we continued to face at the secondary level has been the wide-ranging nature of secondary literacy specialists' work in schools: they might serve as homework helpers, administer literacy programs for an entire school, or teach supplementary literacy classes (Sheehy & Malavasic, 2014). Compounding these challenges has been pressure created by the National Council of Teacher Quality (2013) review to prepare literacy specialists for authentic practices in schools.

In the early years of the Common Core State Standards (CCSS, 2013) implementation, basing teacher preparation programs on current school practices alone was not advisable, but so too was waiting several years to learn what practices are worth authenticating given the onset of the Next Generation Literacy Standards (2017) that continue to place language and literacy within the content areas. As teacher educators, we embraced the ongoing scrutiny that teacher preparation programs have been undergoing and decided that to better align our program with the current middle and high school practices. As such, we anticipated that secondary literacy specialists would benefit from expertise in two areas: course development and teaching the three CCSS emphases—argument, explanation, and narrative. Since narrative reading and writing were supported quite well within other courses in our program, we decided to focus the design of our two-course sequence on curriculum development and teaching argument, often a difficult genre to teach and learn (Shanahan & Shanahan, 2008).

Designing Course 1

Course 1 provides an introductory framework for graduate students and consists of three parts: immersion in knowledge building via literacy events, practice in knowledge building via literacy events, and building a knowledge unit. The students engage with all five literacy events by participating in a unit created and modeled in the prerequisite course taught by Dr. Sheehy. Student use this modeled unit and teach it in small groups within a short, five-hour practicum experience. By the end of Course 1, the graduate students have been involved and assessed all the literacy events within the model knowledge building unit. From there, students apply the structure of the model unit to create their own knowledge units framed within the same theoretical notions as the model unit that they will teach to middle school students via a collaborative inquiry practicum in Course 2, the course represented in this book.

Designing Course 2

Given the above findings and the current direction of research in the field, we determined it appropriate to place the emphasis of Course 2 on the application of teaching argument around the inquiry units and driven by an essential question that has its own literacy demands and has relevance and application across multiple secondary contexts. In dialogical response to the theoretical underpinnings of Course 1, the design of Course 2 aligns with previously noted research that informs the preparation of teachers for work in schools. Hopefully, this book will raise awareness to literacy scholars who are revising curricula and/or developing courses to address these changes.

To adequately address aspects of standards, current research in the field of literacy, and requirements for the preparation of secondary literacy specialists and coaches, the course is divided into two significant sections, a practicum and seminar. The practicum consists of an intense small group inquiry with middle school students using argumentative reading and writing around an essential question.

Emphasis includes creating contexts for inquiry, text selection, responsive reading and writing instruction, discussion, and engaging with families. In the seminar, graduate teachers document and assess students' literacy learning and analyze knowledge built across literacy events via artifacts, instruction, and interactions drawing on theories of literacy development. Within the seminar, graduate teachers develop communities of professional practice as they engage as responsive literacy coaches, analyzing their own and colleagues' teaching interactions, and offering reflections and possibilities for future teaching. Each section will be detailed in subsequent chapters.

Theoretical and Conceptual Frameworks

Knowledge-Building and Cognitive Distribution

The theoretical foundations behind the design of this course via the creation of collaborative literacy inquiry groups are knowledge-building and cognitive distribution. Knowledge-building literacy practices have been explored primarily within content areas such as science studies (Roth, 1997; Zhang & Sun, 2011). While, traditionally, knowledge has been viewed as a fixed and stable property that resides in a person's head, Roth explained (1997) that, in classrooms, students are "engaged in the production of 'knowledgeability' which derives from a community's ongoing practices…[in which] people come to share…conventions, standards, behaviors, viewpoints…through participation" (p. 12). Given the collaborative nature of this course, the framework of knowledge building goes hand in hand with cognitive distribution. Mok (2008) identified cognitive distribution tenets: (1) cognition is not solo, it is distributed across people and artifacts, (2) artifacts are sources of cognition, (3) cognition is socio-cultural and historical, and (4) contexts afford specific cognitive activity. Gallimore and Tharp (1990) referred to cognitive distribution that occurs in interactive teaching through activating schema; assisting performance via modeling, instructing, questioning, and feeding back; and collective knowledge. These frameworks informed the knowledge-building units created by the graduate teachers in a prior prerequisite course that were then implemented with middle school students.

As I noted in the previous chapter, and research such as Nel Noddings (2005) supports, there is a need for adolescents to experience caring relationships in school that are reciprocal and promote classroom communities that are integral to learning. These social interactions are powerful influences on literacy learning along with building relationships and classroom community, two essential keys to successful learning experiences for all students, particularly adolescents (Santa, 2006). It was important to weave the importance of relationship-building throughout the book as this is a central framework of the practicum.

Equally vital was to design the practicum model around the creation of a collaborative teaching community with graduate teachers and middle school students that would encourage teaching as a reciprocal act (Kinloch 2012), where students are seen as active participants in the learning process. By engaging in this framework, graduate teachers come to view themselves as facilitators of the learning and center instruction around opportunities that encourage students to take ownership of their literacy practices to foster literate identities where students see themselves as competent readers and writers. Brozo (2017) reminded us that we are much more likely to sustain the engagement of adolescents as readers and learners if we validate their experiences and capitalize on them to further enhance our classroom culture.

To further conceptualize the model for this course, I cite additional research and theoretical perspectives of adolescence, identity construction, and motivation as they were significant factors among the graduate teachers and middle school students' social interactions and in determining how they might directly link to their [students and teachers] engagements with literacy.

Adolescence: A Time of Change

Adolescents and their experiences have been examined from a variety of different stances. Both theoretical perspectives and popular notions assume some kind of link between physiological changes and the cognitive and affective changes taking place in young people (Moje, 2002). Yet, Finders (1998/1999) and Alvermann (2001, 2009) challenged our traditional understandings of adolescence and caution that the term "adolescence" carries with it some overgeneralizations that limit how we define and think of adolescents and their existing expertise. Ferguson's (2002) research with middle school African-American males contested the view of adolescence as a transitional stage and the conception of adolescents as rebellious, impulsive, and powerless in relationships. She described adolescents as being knowledgeable of teachers' pedagogical practices and "sophisticated participant observers themselves, skilled interpreters and astute analysts of social interactions" (p. 97). She concluded that adolescents can be regarded as "resourceful social actors who [take] an active role in shaping their daily experiences" (p. 15), including literacy learning. Her view suggests that adolescents can be aware of the resources available to them as well as their power to negotiate these sources in their learning. This growing body of research expands our understanding of what it means to be an adolescent and should give us pause to consider our own opinions and assumptions about adolescents.

Constructing and Navigating Identities

Adolescence is a particularly significant phase when young people undergo more rapid and profound changes, particularly related to shifts in their identities, than at any other period in their lives. Stewart Hall (1996) discussed these identity shifts from context to context as a production, emergent in process. Moje (2002) expanded upon his notion when she noted that people, regardless of age, are acting subjects or defined selves who engage in many practices depending upon the spaces, times, and relationships in which they find themselves. This is certainly critical during adolescence where there is an increased urgency for them to construct a sense of identity. This not only includes the way they view themselves, but how others view them.

Adolescent identities shift and change relative to the literacies they use. Their identities are represented and constructed through the literacy practices in which they participate. How one thinks about him/herself is revealed and reshaped as he/she writes and talks—the stories he/she tells reveal identity, are shaped by identity, and shape identity in the process of being told (Sutherland, 2005). Sfard and Prusak (2005) defined identity through narratives to explain identity as a set of stories. Although these stories are often individually told, they are still products of a collective group of people. What is often a difficult task for adolescents is learning to express their identity in a personally meaningful and socially acceptable way. Identity construction can also be a social and political matter because it is an adolescent's struggle to develop a sense of self within a social sphere. Vadeboncoeur and Patel Stevens (2005) argued strongly for considering the social and cultural contexts in which adolescents are constructed, at times decide to replicate themselves, and from time to time challenge or negotiate their way through.

Brian Street (1984) called particular attention to the fact that who people are and how they live makes all the difference in how they learn, how they engage in literacy practices, and the role literacy plays in their identity. As such, adolescent identities are shaped and continually informed by experiences and interactions. Since adolescents spend a major portion of their waking hours in school, schools are both mirrors and shapers of their identity development. In turn, we need to consider how the school structures in place further impact students' identity.

All of these are significant implications for educational practice, and it is important that those who are literacy researchers, teacher educators, and teachers in secondary schools understand the multiple literacy practices adolescents engage in that support their identity construction and how vital interactions and instruction are to identity development. For example, McCarthy (2001) reflecting upon what she observed considers revising our perceptions of students' identities to that of multiple and shifting dependent upon the context to help us better meet the diverse, evolving needs of our students.

I take these aspects of identity construction into account in the design of both the practicum and seminar portions of the course. For example, since research and theory support the notions that teachers' perceptions and beliefs about learners can have an impact on students' thoughts about who they are, a seminar discussion on the multiple facets of identity was vital for graduate teachers to explore how to be self-reflexive about how their own instructional practices are shaped by their identities and lived experiences. To better incorporate this notion, I discuss why choosing to share my own identity web in the first seminar class was a significant step. I then asked each graduate teacher to create and share their own with our seminar group. We discussed how this experience allowed us to gain a better sense each other as people and learn about the multiple identities each of us navigated in the multiple contexts of our lives. For teachers, sharing their webs fostered a critical interrogation of their social locations as a way to consider how they could extend this idea in their collaborative groups to honor students' histories and lives. The identity webs came to be an important factor contributing to the growth of teacher-student relationships.

Adult and adolescent behaviors intersect in many ways, so there is much potential to be gained by increasing awareness of how to further develop these connections through dialogue and learning. There continues to be a need to broaden awareness, particularly among educators who work in secondary contexts, and teacher educators who are preparing teachers to work in secondary contexts as to why identity so powerfully impacts students' learning and their sense of belonging in school. It is through their participation in classroom literacy practices and social interactions that students learn how to negotiate their school lives and relationships with teachers and other students in the class.

Adolescence, Identity Construction, and Literacy

As illustrated in studies of adolescents using literacy, there is a known link between literacy practices and identity construction that can be glimpsed through adolescents' talk about their literacy practices. I know from my previous experiences teaching middle school students how significant the role of projected and recognized identities played in their overall engagement in literacy practices, and school in general. So often students' decisions on their level of class participation were based upon the way the teacher positioned them in the classroom. If teachers examine more closely the reasons why students enact multiple relationships, they can find ways to use these relationships to effect positive academic literacies. As evidenced in the inquiry groups, if students see that teachers respect who they are as people, and realize that teachers care about them, they will want to do well in their academic literacy practices.

There is so much about identity that is crucial to classrooms. Being a successful student requires one to do identity work. Sometimes a student needs to adopt and affiliate with new ways of talking, listening, acting, feeling, responding, interacting, and valuing as well as reading and writing (Gee, 1996) within various classroom spaces. For example, O'Brien (1998, 2006) reflecting on what he had observed in his research with students in an "at risk" high school English program noted that with the creation of literacy labs students were encouraged to explore their identities through popular culture as they wrote letters to newspapers, reviewed movies, and wrote about famous people. The critical point here is students' constructs of identity and motivation to learn are directly linked to the social contexts and relationship that encompass their daily lives. While teachers may not have a large impact upon these social contexts and relationships outside of school, they can create conditions in the classroom that draw upon students' interests and desires that authentic, motivating literacy practices. As Dillon, Moje, and O'Brien (2000) point out, if educators realize that adolescents' ways of knowing, believing, thinking, and acting shape the ways they engage in learning, we are in a better position to tailor our teaching to their strengths and needs. In my experiences in secondary contexts, as well as my daily observations of the collaborative inquiry groups, I have seen adolescents thrive when they are engaged in literacy experiences that are viewed by them as intentional, purposeful, and authentic.

As recent research on secondary youth and motivation by Guthrie, Klauda, and Ho (2013) affirms, teacher-student relationships are considerable factors that contribute to students' motivation and engagement in literacy practices. The result is the belief by students that learning is important and valuable, and if they [students] develop confidence they will become successful. Further research demonstrates an increased focus on understanding youth culture and the complexities around adolescent life in general (Brozo, 2017). Central to all of this is knowing the nature of adolescence, adolescents, and the key to their engagement in literacy practices. This serves to suggest that when students are given opportunities guided by their own curiosity, there are often more occasions for teachers to facilitate and guide learning.

When thinking about motivation and choice, drawing upon students' funds of knowledge was important to consider when thinking about ways to connect resources adolescents bring to school that shape their interests. Scholars such as Moll, Amanti, Neff, and Gonzales (1992) suggested, to be most effective as literacy educators we must recognize the relevant resources within the multiple social contexts within which students operate. It was important to consider motivation as a factor into the inquiry groups. We did this by affording the middle school students the option to rank their interest in the unit topics after they viewed all the presentations by the graduate teachers. Encouraging students to take the lead in which units would be taught was an effective way to balance teacher direction with student choice to further link in and out-of-school literacy interests and resources to the content in the knowledge units. This initiated the roots of community-building and acknowledged early on in the course that student voices were going to be an integral part of the shared, collaborative instruction. The regular responses from the students regarding the process solidify these points.

Concluding Thoughts

When developing any framework, it is crucial for educators to have a vested interest and deep understanding of how research, theory, and practice link together. In the overall organization of this course, I felt it essential to recognize the supportive role research and theory have in informing classroom practices in general, and in particular, the choices I made to adapt to the design and context of this course.

3 Course Components

Practicum Structure and Schedule

The course described in this book is a required course for graduate students seeking to become secondary literacy specialists and coaches. There is a required practicum component for those seeking B-12 or 5–12 certification. This is considered the capstone practicum experience where graduate students are required to complete twenty-five practicum hours working with middle school students. In the practicum portion of the course, graduate teachers work with a teaching partner, share the teaching of the five literacy events within each of three reading cycles, writing workshop, and collaborate on the creation of lesson plans. The groups meet twice a week during the regular semester and is structured according to the following schedule:

4:00–5:30 meet in collaborative inquiry groups
5:30–6:00 meet with families; debriefing, analyzing and reflections, instructional implications
6:00–7:00 seminar discussion around videotaping or class readings

Offering the course afterschool accommodates the schedules of our graduate teachers, many of whom are employed full-time, and affords middle school students access to a unique opportunity to participate in a collaborative learning community with a range of literacy events and knowledge building that extends beyond the school context, and one that is designed to further bridge the in-school and out-of-school literacies of middle school students.

As a teacher educator and former middle school reading specialist, I have seen the value of university/school partnerships to all stakeholders involved such as students, teachers, families, administrators, and the school community. One of the things we do in the course to prepare graduate teachers for their practicum experience is review the school website and mission statement. It is important for graduate teachers to learn about the school environment and students so they can position themselves within these contexts and feel they are a part of the school community albeit for only a semester. However, I should note that in the past, I have had graduate students hired for teaching jobs upon graduation as a result of their experiences within the practicum course.

Frameworks for Teaching and Learning

Daily Seminars

Although the majority of the semester takes place at the school, another significant aspect of the course are the daily seminars. Prior to the start of the practicum experience, the seminars encompass the entire three hours of class. During the first four-five days of the course, the students and I convene in a small group setting where we engage in readings, discussions, and writing. This experience centers around creating a mindset about the importance of teaching teachers how to construct learning communities built around trust and respect for each other that will expand their perspectives, conversations, and reflections as they engage as future literacy specialists and coaches. As a group, we read and focus our discussions on literature that incorporates research, theory, and practice. I select the literature to inform and organize thinking and prompt critical discussions that demonstrate how teachers are reflecting upon and changing their practices.

For example, one of our initial conversations is related to the general discourse regarding adolescents. Often students in our B-12 program have limited or no experience engaging with adolescents prior to taking this course. To ease what can sometimes be an anxiety-producing experience for them, we read and discuss assumptions about adolescents, media and academic representations of adolescents, and ways to better understand the lived experiences of adolescents. We explore initiatives in adolescent literacy such as Reading Next (2004) and Writing Next (2007) and develop a graphic organizer to compare and contrast the various aspects highlighted in each. We discuss how each initiative expands the foundation to inform and continues to inform the teaching of adolescents and adolescent literacy.

We delve deeper and examine two other initiatives, The International Literacy Association Adolescent Literacy Position Statement

(2012) and Standards for Reading Professionals (2017) to broaden our conversations in a more global perspective, further understand the instructional implications of the shifts in standards, and how as future literacy educators they can envision how literacy instruction is taken upon in an array of global contexts. For example, in one of our discussions, we expand our understandings around the implication for instruction based upon the notion raised in the International Literacy Association Position Statement (2012) that adolescents are "global citizens who make up a diverse range of linguistic, cultural, and socioeconomic backgrounds who engage in multiple forms of literacy" (p. 2). We discuss how this could address different cultural expectations that shape the multiple ways adolescents choose to enact identities, and how the context of this course can help us expand these notions through engaging adolescents in literacy experiences centered around social interactions and content that include different forms of media.

From the beginning of the course, I emphasize the importance of language since it is central to the social interactions and instruction taking place in the collaborative groups. A substantial part of our own learning community considers ways of thinking and rethinking language in all aspects of our work as teachers and learners. As future literacy specialists and coaches, we focus on ways to embed language into our conversations based upon the framework of Gallimore and Tharp (1990). Through seminar discussions, we develop working definitions of the terms noted and begin to practice applying them as we analyze samples of teaching scripts. This dialogue is intended to encourage reflection from the perspective of a literacy coach in identifying the language patterns occurring within the lessons and to gradually embed them in their day-to-day interactions and conversations as teachers and coaches. This is a critical step to develop over time to ensure interactions and dialogue with colleagues not be viewed in a judgmental or evaluative manner (Figure 3.1).

This literature also serves as the basis to develop our own professional learning community with a common discourse. It is important to devote time to cultivate a professional learning community prior to the graduate teachers' work with middle school students. Working in a small group setting establishes a space for future discussions structured to ensure that participate and their voices are equally heard. Having opportunities for this collaborative thinking and learning enables graduate teachers to realize their own capability for producing these kinds of conversations. It also enhances their awareness of their own social location and how that positions

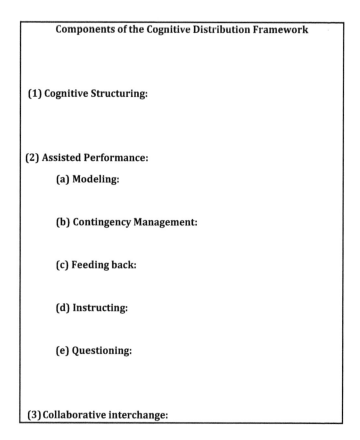

Figure 3.1 Cognitive distribution framework terminology sheet.

them as teachers working with students, colleagues, families, and the school community.

During these first few days, everyone has a chance to review the content of the knowledge unit topics each teacher developed in the prerequisite course to familiarize them with all the topics in the event they teach a unit topic they did not create. Not every graduate teacher took the prerequisite course at the same time, so each works individually to develop the key instructional components of their knowledge units and design a digital unit presentation they will share the first day they meet with the middle school students. Each teacher shares the presentation in class with colleagues who provide constructive feedback via thoughtful language intended to inform the final product before it is presented to the students.

Ongoing Professional Development

There is a distinct feature of the course that links professional development to literacy coaching. As Elish-Piper, L'Allier, Manderino, and DiDomenico (2016) reminded us, there are many unique challenges when working as a literacy coach in secondary settings. At this level, literacy coaches must wear many hats in their day-to-day interactions with teachers. To further enhance our professional learning community and address the future leadership roles associated with being a literacy coach, each set of teaching partners engage as discussion facilitators in seminar incorporating material from a selected reading from our coaching text. The discussion is designed to extend and enrich the course inquiries and to help the class summarize and synthesize knowledge.

As part of the assignment, teaching partners create a handout they will use to guide the small group conversations. On the handout they note main ideas, compelling examples of data such as quotes and excerpts, and teaching implications they gleaned from the reading around literacy research, theory, and practice. They develop two-three key essential questions that serve as the basis for multiple conversations. I have found these conversations to be a fundamental tool in the course to enable teachers to learn how to take a productive and active role in their learning along with that of their colleagues. The conversations are also intended to inform collaborative thinking and prepare teachers to take up these same roles in future educational settings.

Reimagining and Revisiting Components of the Knowledge Units

As previously noted, in the prerequisite course, each graduate teacher creates a knowledge unit designed around an essential question in a prerequisite course. The knowledge units include three different reading cycles each using multimodal texts from multiple perspectives taught within five literacy events (Heath, 1983): word work, guided reading and discussion, seminar and quick writes, and writing workshop.

When creating these units, graduate teachers developed an essential question around a controversial issue relevant to middle school-age students; chose texts both print and digital that would help students form an argument inclusive of claim, counterclaim, and evidence; determined what "foot-in-the-door" words were central to the content; considered how guided reading should be taught; designed writing-to-learn artifacts (e.g., two-sided notes); and created Socratic seminar and quick write prompts. They chose a clear argument that they would read closely using sub-questions and multiple readings for each of the three different reading cycles. For example, one reading may focus on organization, another on argument development using claim and counterclaim, and another on language development.

During the writing workshop, each middle school student determines his/her stance on the issue and completes a written argument around the essential question reflected in their unit. Finally, each student selects a culminating digital project such as a Glog, Prezi, movie, etc., and design a presentation that expands upon the claim, counterclaim, and evidence noted in their written argument piece. The students share these projects publicly with their families who are invited by the students to attend a celebration on the last day of the course. Chapter 7 discusses the family celebration in detail.

Description of Literacy Events

Word Work

Teachers determine 3–4 words unknown to the students and of significance to the overall comprehension of the text. They initially teach the words to the students with explicit instruction via modeling and scaffolds such as vocabulary frames, four-square graphic organizers. As the group engages in each reading, they revisit the words when they appear in the text with the purpose being to reinforce understanding of the word in the context of the reading.

Guided Reading and Discussion

As previously discussed, lessons follow the I Do, We Do, framework. These literacy events involve a close reading of the text using artifacts such as double-sided notes, annotations, etc., framed around discussion prompts using accountable talk stems designed to pull literal evidence from the text, draw inferences from the text, or use personal connections for application to the text.

Shared Reading and Partner Discussion

Upon completing text readings, group members pair up (teacher-teacher, teacher-student, or student-student) and use their notes for a shared discussion of the readings. This provides an opportunity to expand upon each other's ideas and take-aways from the readings and prepare their claim and counterclaim arguments for the Socratic Seminar.

Socratic Seminar

Participants engage in this literacy event as a team with their partner from the previous discussion. The first team presents their opening stance/claim and supportive evidence using the accountable talk stems. The second team follows with their counterclaim and supportive evidence in the same manner. The seminar continues until each team has fully debated their argument.

Writing

Writing occurs at various times throughout each reading cycle such as, a quick write to summarize the overall points from the Socratic Seminar, or as an interactive summary writing where the entire inquiry group synthesizes their learning.

Reading Cycles

Each of the three reading cycles is generally divided into four days. In order to give the reader a full sense of the unit design, this first sample unit details the events on day one that involves the entire class (teachers and students) in team-building activities, followed by graduate teachers' presentations of their knowledge unit topics. On day two, the knowledge unit topics are determined based upon the middle school students' rankings and the small groups are formed. The remainder of the time is spent on ice-breaker activities and sharing identity webs. As I previously noted, unique to the success of the collaborative learning communities is the focus on forming teacher-student relationships, devoting time for teachers and students to learn about each other, and establishing a discourse to talk about teaching and learning within the inquiry groups prior to digging into the content of the knowledge unit (Figure 3.2).

Knowledge Building Unit Calendar	
Session 1 of Week	*Session 2 of Week*
Day 1 Get to Know Students	Day 2 Unit "Sell"
Day 3 Pre-Assessments • GRADE? • DRP? Writing • May make up a self-assessment	Day 4 Text 1: On the Same Team? The Debate Over Youth Co-ed Sports (Introduces controversy)
Day 5 Text 2: What are the benefits of Girls and Boys playing sports on the same team? (Pros) Seminar Prompts: -Why are coed sports controversial? -Why is Title IX important for athletes? -Build the claim, "Schools should have coed sports."	Day 6 Text 3: Are There Disadvantages of Girls and Boys Playing Together in Sports? (Cons) Writing

Figure 3.2 Excerpt from unit addressing the question: Should sports be coed?

The second sample unit provides an overview of the first reading cycle structure and opens with the overarching question: Should schools be able to limit students' first amendment rights? The first cycle of this particular unit includes two texts for guided reading and discussions, three vocabulary words that are taught via explicit instruction in word work, quick writes that are responses to a short prompt generated from the guided discussions, partner discussions using notes from the two guided readings, and a Socratic Seminar focused on a specific sub-question related to the overall essential question for the topic (Figure 3.3).

The First Amendment at School

Essential Question: Content
1. Should schools be able to limit students First Amendment rights?

Essential Questions: Literacy
1. How do readers determine the validity of an author's claim and the evidence supporting them?
2. How do writers make clear claims and support them with evidence?
3. How do students grow ideas in discussion?

Culminating Essay
Argument: A final written argument, inclusive of an introduction to the problem, a claim, support for the claim, at least one counterclaim and reasons for it, a rebuttal, and a conclusion.
Culminating Project
Argument: present the argument using a digital platform.

At a Glance Calendar Plan

A. Orientation: Days 1 and 2

Day 1

1. Teachers get to know students
2. Students listen to unit talks and rank favorites

Reading Cycle One
Topic: Background on the First Amendment and its application to Public Schools

DAY 1
1. Introduction to Unit
A. What is a claim/counterclaim?
Lesson: (video clips of claim/counters and discuss, etc.)
B. Introduce the unit: walk students through the texts and discuss the essential questions.
C. Set literacy goals with student (Possible goals: take notes to help close reading comprehension; use note-taking to make connections between facts in text; work on elaborating topic sentences and supporting information in Quick Writes and Summary Writing...)

Figure 3.3 Excerpt from unit addressing the question: Should schools be able to limit students' first amendment rights?

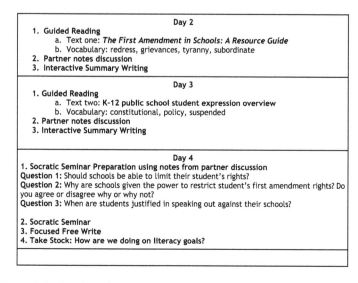

Day 2
1. Guided Reading
a. Text one: *The First Amendment in Schools: A Resource Guide*
b. Vocabulary: redress, grievances, tyranny, subordinate
2. Partner notes discussion
3. Interactive Summary Writing

Day 3
1. Guided Reading
a. Text two: K-12 public school student expression overview
b. Vocabulary: constitutional, policy, suspended
2. Partner notes discussion
3. Interactive Summary Writing

Day 4
1. Socratic Seminar Preparation using notes from partner discussion
Question 1: Should schools be able to limit their student's rights?
Question 2: Why are schools given the power to restrict student's first amendment rights? Do you agree or disagree why or why not?
Question 3: When are students justified in speaking out against their schools?
2. Socratic Seminar
3. Focused Free Write
4. Take Stock: How are we doing on literacy goals?

Figure 3.3 (Continued).

The samples in this chapter represent sections of the units to give the reader a sense of the overall structure and provide an outline of each day's events. Details of each lesson component and literacy event descriptions are written on the daily lesson plan template discussed in Chapter 4.

4   Changing Worlds of the Reading Specialist/ Literacy Coach

Defining/Redefining Roles

The overarching intent and design of this course is to prepare graduate students to become literacy specialists and coaches. Thus, before detailing the rationale behind the particular components in this section, it is beneficial to briefly note some background on the evolving titles and roles of literacy specialists and coaches and how this informs the course components. As Lambert (1998) suggested, there should be an ongoing emphasis in schools on shared leadership, in which school personnel are "learning together, and constructing meaning and knowledge collectively and collaboratively" (p. 5). Given the various roles they assume may vary, most specialist and coaches will take part in some form of instructional support through coaching and leadership. In order to effectively engage in these roles specialists and coaches must exhibit leadership, interpersonal, and communication skills that will enable them to work effectively in schools as they exist today (Bean, 2015).

Along with the supportive roles, it is noteworthy to mention how language in the literacy field has been developed to more clearly define the role of a literacy coach. For example, Toll (2005) defined a literacy coach as

> one who helps teachers to recognize what they know and can do, assists teachers as they strengthen their ability to make more effective use of what they know and do, and supports teachers as they learn more and do more.
>
> (p. 4)

Almost a decade later, a revised definition by Toll (2014) contained noticeable shifts in language, "A literacy coach partners with teachers for job-embedded professional learning that enhances teachers' reflections on students, the curriculum, and pedagogy for the purpose of more effective decision-making" (p. 10). I felt it important to include this terminology as it characterizes language I used as the basis for my descriptions to represent the role of literacy coaches in this course.

Teaching and Coaching for Reflection and Analysis

The tools and related assignments described in this chapter are designed to engage graduate teachers first as reflective practitioners. Being self-reflective encourages teachers to examine themselves as teachers, learners, and observers while they engage in interactions with students and teaching partners in the inquiry groups. Second, to assist teachers to become observant literacy coaches in the context of individual and collaborative observation.

In both instances, the assignments and tools described in this chapter are intended to help teachers identify and expand upon what they know and can do as teachers, and to bolster their ability to support their colleagues as they continue to learn.

Debriefing and Reflecting: Lesson Plans

One aspect that documents teaching is within structured daily lesson plans teaching partners create together. These lesson plans provide the teachers with a specific routine and timeframe to construct the literacy events they will teach each day. Each lesson details the instructional components, readings, writings, and artifacts that will be required during the ninety-minute session. There are certain sections that teaching partners complete prior to the start of each lesson, and in some instances, these are informed by the reflections, literacy event analyses, and implications from the previous day's lesson plan. Although the overall structure of the lesson plan consists of a Before (I Do), During (We Do), and After (You Do) format, graduate teachers also use these lesson plans to document the teaching-learning observations that take place as throughout the lesson. Figure 4.1 is the template of the lesson plan used for this documentation.

Below are descriptions of the purpose and content of the various categories within the lesson plan.

Topic/Content/Rationale

Teachers use this section to highlight the literacy events that will be taught on the given day including specific dialogue, prompts, and language teachers will use to introduce each literacy event.

Lesson Plan Date_____

Topic/Content: Give a 1-2 sentence description of the lesson.

Rationale: (a) Describe how the lesson will be introduced. Include the literacy events. (b) Describe how the students will participate. Artifacts: List the texts, tools, etc. that will be used during the lesson.

Before: Describe the preliminary vocabulary word work or teaching required, and/or modeling of how to read the tool(s) you will be using.

During: (a) Describe the active reading and activities along with what you will be doing. (b) Describe how the students will be actively reading/thinking while reading (going from I do to We do). (c) Describe the plan for student independent work (going from We do to You do).

After: Note the connections and implications that inform the next lesson.

Writing: (a) Describe the writing you chose and what you will do. (b) Describe how the students will be actively thinking and writing. (c) Describe the plan for independent writing.

After: Complete the literacy event analysis chart using your observation logs and reflections of the lesson to describe the knowledge built within each literacy event throughout each day's lesson. Describe the implications and directions for the next lesson based upon your understandings of the students as learners so far.

Figure 4.1 Lesson plan instructional planning sheet.

Artifacts

Here teachers specify the artifacts that will be used during the lesson. These include texts, media, and tools such as graphic organizers. This information is later transferred to a literacy event chart that teachers share with their teaching partners to analyze the knowledge shifts that occurred during the events of the day's lesson.

Word Work

In this section, teachers include the mini-lessons and introduce the tool(s) used to explicitly model and scaffold vocabulary. Here the instructor would look for a rationale explaining why these are appropriate choices and asking teachers to articulate their instructional decisions.

Guided Reading/Strategic Teaching

It should be noted that this heading applies to both the reading and writing events that take place within each reading cycle. Parts of this particular section are completed prior to the teaching. Teachers formulate initial prompts along with strategies, dialogical discussions, and language they envision students using while actively engaging in the various literacy events either from being prompted or independently. Discussion prompts have included, "Why do you believe there are either benefits or limits for participating on coed sports teams?" "Describe a section from the reading that supports your point." These prompts can be applied to either a guided discussion of a reading, or to a quick write/discussion. Throughout the semester, as teachers further analyze the interactions, instruction, and artifacts during their audio and video analyses this section is further developed as teachers become much more strategic and their comments expand in detail. This is particularly evident after teachers and students engage in more dialogical conversations within the collaborative inquiry groups via partner discussions and Socratic Seminar. Another factor sparking these shifts is the level of teacher-student bonds beginning to develop within the learning community. For example, Barb notes how learning about her students' interests in and out-of-school supports the connections they made during the group discussions:

> As we engaged in discussions during each event in our lesson,
> we learned more about our students' interests and strengths

as learners. As a learner, Jim creates connections to his own experiences and to the texts he reads to support the different perspectives of each group member has shared. As a learner, Morgan engages the group in a critical discussion through questioning and building upon connections to the perspectives each group member shares.

Observation Logs

As previously noted, throughout the practicum portion of the course, graduate teachers engage as both a teacher and a literacy coach. In the role of literacy coach, they observe their partner teaching and the group interactions taking place during each lesson. Teachers are expected to use an observation log to record supportive evidence that includes what they notice from the lesson in the form of excerpts, quotes, and/or comments from both teachers and students addressing specific areas. A sample observational log is included below. The areas included for observation directly apply the terms previously shown in Figure 4.2.

Cognitive Structuring

In this section, teachers observe and note how they are using explanations, strategies, and instructional decisions to activate schema and build background knowledge for their students.

Literacy Coaching Observation Log (include excerpts and quotes)
Name_____Date_____

Cognitive Structuring	Assisted Performance	Collaborative Interchange
Activating schema, instructional decisions	Modeling, Feeding back, Instructing, Questioning	Students and/or teachers building knowledge from each others' interpretations or experiences

Figure 4.2 Observation log.

Assisted Performance

In their theory of assisted performance, Gallimore and Tharp (1990) discussed principles they view as critical in guiding the design of social organizations, such as our collaborative inquiry groups, to foster the teaching and learning of all members. Within this principle is a set of five distinct categories, modeling, contingency management, feeding back, instructing, and questioning.

Modeling

This attends to the way teachers demonstrate desired behaviors then provide scaffolds for the students to imitate these behaviors independently.

Contingency Management

Here teachers engage in response to interactions among teachers and/or students focused on reinforcing positive behaviors using praise and encouraging language, stickers, food, etc.

Feeding Back

Although somewhat similar to contingency management, feeding back is a response to instruction that involves ongoing interactions and dialogue. For example, in contingency management a teacher may respond to a student using encouraging language such as, I noticed you effectively used evidence to support your claim. The conversation would end. Yet, in feeding back, there would be a continued dialogue where the student would respond to the teacher. This same type of dialogue could also occur within peer-to-peer interactions in the group.

Instructing

Here teachers contemplate how they are using instructional language to guide students through the various tasks.

Questioning

This section requires teachers to focus on the nature of the questions being asked and calls for an active response from the learner, either verbal or cognitive such as a nod.

Collaborative Interchange

Given the collaborative nature of the learning community, this area is acknowledged by having teachers note evidence that shows how students and/or teachers are building knowledge from each other via interpretations or experiences. An important aspect of documenting teaching occurs through debriefing immediately after each teaching session. Teaching partners meet to share, reflect upon, and analyze their observational logs to determine what shifts in knowledge occurred, and what factors such as artifacts, instruction, and/or interactions may have influenced those shifts. Although the notations on the logs and the conversations related to them are sometimes superficial in the beginning of the course, they become more focused, thoughtful, and memorable as teachers learn to become more attentive to the instruction, interactions, and artifacts, that are shifting the collective knowledge in the group. After repeated experiences writing and conversing, teachers also see the value in using these analytic tools.

Literacy Event Charts

During the lesson debriefing time, teachers expand conversations and connections from their observation logs in combination with lesson plans to further extend the discussion of the day's lesson and inform future instruction. The literacy events graphic organizer takes the analysis one step further and becomes an effective tool to reflect upon and document the knowledge building that occurred across the literacy events taught in each lesson, and how these have informed and continue to inform the teaching of literacy from guided reading to small group discussion to Socratic Seminar.

Teachers use three columns to chart evidence from each lesson noting the literacy event, artifact, and knowledge-building that occurred within each event. For example, during guided reading graduate students analyze the ideas built within the event, the level of comprehension that is demonstrated by the students as they move from the modeling (teacher demos to students) to scaffolds (teacher and students work together) to independent work (students read and take notes), and whether this level is aligned to each task. They conduct the same analysis when the instruction shifts from individual notes to a small group discussion where students share their notes and understandings. A template of the literacy event chart currently used is shown in Figure 4.3. Figure 4.4 represents a cross section from Kathy's literacy event

Reading Cycle #__________ **Date**______________________________

Literacy Event	Artifact	Knowledge Building

Figure 4.3 Literacy event planning sheet.

3/29	Supplemental Text (cheerleading)	- annotation chart - cheerleading text	Application info from previous texts on football Interpretive: Own experiences
4/10	T-chart	- text 5/6 - cheerleading text	Application: Connected texts together to build on ideas Literal: pulling evidence from text and writing on sticky notes Interpretive: Discussed info to add, whether it would support advantage or disadvantage
4/12	Practice Argumentative Writing	- Texts 1–6 - T-chart - Planning Sheet - 6 hooks Sheet	Application: Applying evidence from texts that connects to claim Interpretive: Thought of how to grab audience attention by posing possible scenarios (set a scene hook) Literal: used outline from planning sheet
4/12	Socratic Seminar	- T-chart - Texts 1–6 - Talk stems - Supplemental texts	Application: Used talk stems and referred to T-chart/texts for evidence ~~[illegible]~~ Inferential: used texts/T-chart for evidence in order to pose questions

Figure 4.4 Excerpt from Kathy's literacy event sheet.

chart to show how she documented the shifts in students' knowledge using artifacts such as a supplemental text reading, T-Chart and literacy events such as writing, and Socratic Seminar.

Video Analysis

Video analysis is one example that demonstrates how teachers engage in teaching and learning interactions and dialogue through the lens of a literacy coach. A significant part of the process involves teacher engagement in conversations designed to provide constructive, written feedback to one another and to offer suggestions for future instruction. Twice during the seminar portion of the course, each graduate teacher selects and presents a ten-minute videotaped segment of his/her explicit teaching around a specific literacy event. Teachers are asked to select a segment from the lesson that demonstrates rich knowledge building teacher instructional language and responsive student language that supports evidence of student engagement. The video segments are purposely selected with the first occurring during the beginning of the collaborative groups, while the second is done toward the end of the course. In both instances, the videotaped experiences lead the teachers to notice, analyze, and provide feedback to their teaching colleagues and detail the observations of their own teaching practices.

The teacher being observed manages and frames the presentation while the remaining class members take on the role of literacy coaches. To introduce the video segment to their colleagues, each teacher distributes a written narrative that overviews the content and explains why they selected the video as an effective example. This narrative is generally one page single-spaced in length. The narrative includes (a) a brief description of students, (b) an overview of the literacy events and specific content in the lesson, and (c) three areas/ questions for their colleagues to consider related to what they are noticing about the instruction, interactions, and/or artifacts as they view the video. This also serves as a way to further prompt reflective discussion. Making this selection does place the presenter in somewhat of a vulnerable position, yet at the same time looking forward to and seeking the trusting feedback from fellow colleagues that can be used for future analysis and interpretation of teaching practice.

While they view the video, all class members take on the role of a literacy coach making notations to address the presenters' questions and based upon their observations conducting an analysis utilizing language that reflects knowledge building through cognitive distribution. After each video presentation, all teachers participate in a discussion facilitated by the observed teacher. Each teacher uses notes to focus comments extending upon examples that demonstrate the instructional language they observed from their colleague that informed knowledge building and cognition distributed among the teacher and students. Each observed teacher collects the written viewing notes from her teaching colleagues and includes examples from the notes in a separate written analysis of each video that addresses the following:

a   Describe the evidence of student knowledge building (shifts in thinking, changes in language, acknowledging new perspectives) in each video. Use at least three comments or quotes, from the viewing notes and seminar discussion as evidence to support.
b   Describe any shifts in your own knowledge building evident in your video.
c   What stood out as significant and/or what might you do differently? Why?
d   What new learning did you take from this experience and from your colleagues written comments and the class discussion that you will implement in your next lesson(s)?
e   Supplemental documents: Include both the written explanation of your video (from #1), and the notes from your colleagues (from #2) with your analysis.

The following document shows a section from Julie's written analysis of her first video presentation. In her reflection, Julie commented on the value of the experience and the insights gleaned from her colleagues:

The coaching portion of this experience fostered my growth as a professional because I listened to the feedback from my colleagues. They identified effective language that I used to engage students in conversation, pushing them to think beyond the cell phone policies. The non-judgmental atmosphere supports a natural conversation where my colleagues aren't afraid to be honest and give constructive suggestions. From my colleagues' written comments and class discussion, I learned that I asked productive questions, especially when I asked what parts of the cell phone policy students in our group would change.

The second video is presented in the same manner as discussed above, but for the analysis teachers draw upon the previous video analysis and add to their discussion the following:

a   Describe the student-to-student and student-to-teacher interactions you observed.

b   Describe to what degree (greatly, somewhat, slightly) your instructional choices contributed to shifts in students' knowledge levels and language choices in both videos.

The following document shows a segment from Julie's second video analysis. Here, she discussed more detailed observations and supportive evidence of her teaching practices and how they further impacted students' understanding.

After analyzing and discussing both videos with my colleagues, I noticed that my language and questioning informed the many shifts in the students' level of knowledge. During Reading Cycle #1, the initial encouragement of accountable talk stems supported student engagement in discussions. The students consciously decided whether to agree, disagree, and/or add on to their peer's insights by referring to the stems on the table. During the third reading cycle, the students seamlessly include accountable talk stems in their discussions and did not need to refer to the initial accountable talk stem handout. During the first cycle, I asked open-ended questions such as *"What did you notice about what we said to each other?"* During reading cycle three, my questions continued to push the students to think above and beyond the texts. I asked each student *"What are your thoughts?"*, *"What would you change about the cell phone policies and why?"*, and *"Do you think the policies are fair? Why or why not?"* Based on my overall analysis of both videos, I determined the students' level of knowledge, and language choice has grown in leaps and bounds since the first cycle.

Throughout the videotaped discussions, teachers have an opportunity to observe an array of teacher-student interactions, artifacts, and teaching strategies they can apply to their future teaching. I regularly hear positive comments from the teachers regarding this process as being significant to their development as acute observers of their own instruction and interactions with students, and in the case of this class, shifts in the level and quality of the collaborative interactions among members of the inquiry groups.

Audio Analysis of Knowledge Building through Self-Reflection

Although the teachers engage as literacy coaches and gain regular feedback during the videotaped segments, another significant part of the course requires teachers to learn how to give this same feedback to themselves. To foster this proficiency, graduate teachers complete an audiotaped analysis of their own teaching. Graduate teachers select and analyze a transcribed segment of their teaching that demonstrates how their instructional interactions and language were used to support students using rich knowledge-building instructional language and student language that is evidence of student engagement.

The audiotape analysis is completed during reading cycle two and encourages teachers to self-reflect upon the nature of their interactions and the implications for instruction. Graduate teachers select a ten-minute segment that best demonstrates what they determine to be an excerpt containing rich knowledge building language among teacher and students within the collaborative groups.

The first layer of analysis involves competing a three-page, single-spaced written transcription of the audiotaped segment. It begins with a brief (three- to four-sentence) overview of the lesson including a description of the context of the lesson, why the particular lesson was chosen, and the preparation, planning, and artifacts chosen and organized for the lesson. Within the written transcriptions, teachers engage as reflective practitioners using a different color, font, or handwritten notes to annotate/analyze language choices, teaching practices in their transcript citing three distinct areas: (a) evidence of students' knowledge building (e.g., language, questioning), (b) examples of responses to student engagement, and (c) evidence of shifts in their own knowledge building (e.g. language, questioning, instruction).

The concluding section requires teachers to cite three specific excerpts and information to support their analysis to address the following questions:

a   What went well in the lesson based upon the evidence of student learning?
b   What role did your instructional interactions and language play in student learning?
c   What might you do differently as a result?

The following is a segment from Angela's analysis of her audiotape transcription. Here she applies the knowledge she has gained about the collaborative interactions within her group, and the understandings she has acquired as a result:

> Within our group, all forms of collaborative interchange took place, student-teacher, student-student, and teacher-teacher.

In the beginning of the lesson as we were reading from one of the texts, a student asked, "What does rhetorical mean?" I responded back to the student by explaining, "It means someone is not expecting an answer back from a question." I was trying to think of a specific example, when one of my colleagues in the group jumped in reaffirming its meaning by saying, "Someone is asking you a question, but is not looking for an answer back." The teacher gave another example of a rhetorical question by asking, "Are you serious?" The teachers contributed to explaining what rhetorical meant, so the student was able to not only hear the definition phrased in different ways, but also heard an example she could use to connect the word in real life. After she heard the example, the student nodded her head. I am confident that this conversation left her with complete understanding of the word.

In my experiences teaching the course, I have found that some graduate teachers express a preference for the audiotape while others prefer the videotape. However, all find each analysis particularly helpful in gauging their language use, interactions with students and colleagues, and teaching practices. Along with beneficial reflective analysis for the students, these transcriptions afford myself, as the instructor, with useful ways to build upon additional conversations about my daily observations around the teacher's interactions with students and colleagues within the collaborative groups.

Knowledge Building Assessment: Documenting Teaching and Learning

After completing reading cycle two, the teachers are required to complete a mini-analysis of their teaching and learning during the halfway point of the course. Engaging in this assignment encourages teachers to step away from their collaborative groups and integrate their learning experiences thus far in the course. In their reflective analysis, they compare data from all the literacy events taught within the first two reading cycles. They incorporate the data to document, reflect, and discuss students' and their own learning of the various literacy events. They also examine the shifts in knowledge that occurred and the role that interactions, instructions, and artifacts played in contributing to those shifts. For this assignment, they cannot simply make assertions without citing evidence to justify them. They are required to se-lect a minimum of four excerpts from lesson plan reflections and/ or coaching logs as evidence to support the claims they present in their narrative. Documenting using data assists the teachers in re-examining their choices of instructional practices and ar-tifacts to determine how these both shape and are shaped by the interactions occurring within the collaborative inquiry groups. The paper is usually four-six pages double-spaced and addresses the following questions:

1   Reading Cycle 1 (describe the literacy events in the cycle)

   a   What type of knowledge did the students build in each event (literal, interpretive, and/or application knowledge)? How did knowledge change or get used differently across events? (Cite an example to support.)

   b   How did you as a teacher engage students within these literacy events? Describe the roles of teachers and students in the dis-cussions and the type of information that was shared by each. What were some of the instructional strategies, language choices, and tools you used? (Cite an example to support.)

2   Reading Cycle 2 (describe the literacy events in the cycle)

   a   Answer the same question as above. (Cite an example to support.)

   b   Describe any changes in the discussions, instructional strategies, language, or tools since the end of cycle 1. What factors contributed to these changes? If there were no changes overall, why? (Cite an example to support.)

The first example from Julie's narrative demonstrates the effect of the interactions between she and her colleague as they modeled ac-countable talk.

In reading cycle one, the interactions were mostly teacher-to-teacher. At the beginning, my colleague and I modeled accountable talk stems and shared reading, which required us engage in conversations with each other as we interacted with the reading. For example, I said, "As I read, I noticed that the arti-cle used specific data to inform us of how cell phones can be a distraction. It says...." Then Angela replied, "I am going to use this accountable talk stem 'I agree' to start my response to Miss J. Miss J., I agree with your statement. I also noticed these statistics.

I found it alarming that...." We paired with the students and used scaffolds for them to apply during their discussions and Socratic Seminar. Incorporating this type of modeling for accountable talk and giving positive feedback when students used the language was effective for the students as they applied it during each subsequent lesson.

In the second example, Julie expands her narrative to explain the emerging shifts in roles, language, and reflective thinking she noticed during a conversation between the students in her group.

In the second reading cycle, many of the interactions were student-to-student based. I noticed the students started to assume more of the teacher role in partner discussions and Socratic Seminar. One student led the conversation by noting that, "Studies say students go on cell phones for unrelated reasons."

Another student replied, "The fourth paragraph says the average student may be distracted for 2/3 of a school year. That's not good."

Then the first student noted,

> In the other article, it seems like they really don't want phones. They don't even consider the pros/benefits. They were talking about the real- life example where the girl got a six-page text and that doesn't seem like a good idea during the school day.

This interaction demonstrates the students' language shifts from general ideas to referring to specific facts in multiple articles. My colleague and I purposely did not jump into the conversation because we felt the students' easily built knowledge without our involvement.

Longitudinal Knowledge Building Analysis and Reflection

At the end of the semester, graduate teachers write a comprehensive longitudinal narrative synthesizing and analyzing the knowledge building that occurred across all three reading cycles along with the role artifacts, interactions, and instruction played in these shifts. Writing this paper requires teachers to draw upon the multitude of data they have collected from teaching and coaching in the inquiry groups, student work, lesson plans, logs, literacy event charts, and seminar discussions. This reflective paper encourages teachers use their data from the entire semester to discuss the interactions, instruction, and artifacts (tools) in the course that have had the greatest impact upon the knowledge building of their inquiry group students and of themselves and how and why these were central to the knowledge shifts that occurred.

They submit a final reflective paper based upon their teaching of the entire knowledge unit citing specific evidence using three examples from each of the three reading cycles to support the narrative. This paper is usually six-eight double-spaced pages in length and addresses the following questions:

1   Overall, what did you learn about how to use literacy events to build knowledge? Which events were most effective in shifting students' knowledge levels and why? (Cite a specific example from each reading cycle as evidence.)
2   What did your students learn from your instruction? What were the most effective instructional strategies and/or language choices and why? (Cite a specific example from each reading cycle as evidence.)
3   What were the most effective instructional resources, artifacts and texts (print and digital) that informed students' shifts in knowledge during the entire unit? (Cite a specific example from each reading cycle as evidence.)
4   Describe the shifts in your own levels of knowledge and/or language and instruction that occurred as a result of teaching this unit? What factors may have contributed to these shifts?

In the first example, Barb describes how she and her teaching partner effectively modeled, then collaborated with their students to create vocabulary frames to support students' understanding of the text.

A literacy event that we introduced within the first reading cycle was a vocabulary frame. While my teaching partner and I created vocabulary frames alongside the students during the first lesson in order to support their comprehension, we also modeled how to apply the vocabulary frames throughout the reading of a text. We used vocabulary frames to help our students build their literal and inferential knowledge as they wrote down the definition to the vocabulary word in one corner of the card, and then used that definition to infer its meaning through the use of an illustration, antonym, and sentence including the word. The vocabulary frames they created support their knowledge building as they applied these frames during the reading of the text to develop a deeper comprehension of the author's main idea. For example, prior to reading a paragraph in text one I explained,

This paragraph starts with one of our vocabulary words, competence. Let's look back at the vocabulary frame and review the word. We wrote that this word means the ability to do something successfully and the antonym is failure. So, in this paragraph they are saying that boys accept success over failure, so they will take girls on their team who play better than a guy.

In another section of her paper, she further details the value of using the vocabulary frames in her analysis of this artifact within all three reading cycles. She notes the significant behaviors and patterns that produced learning for all members of the group and considers the areas of her teaching that needed reconsideration during the subsequent reading cycle.

One shift in knowledge that I noticed for my teaching partner and myself throughout the unit was our incorporation of the vocabulary frames within our text-based discussions, readings, and Socratic Seminars. Within the first reading cycle, we focused on the vocabulary words and frames prior to the readings and discussions, but we did not refer back to the frames throughout the reading. During reading cycle two, we shifted this application by referencing the vocabulary frame after reading the paragraph that the vocabulary word was in. The group member who created the vocabulary frame shared their frame and then referred back to the sentence in the text, putting it into their own words, in order to support the group members' comprehension of the text. Within our discussions, we noticed our incorporation of the vocabulary words based on the students' responses. For example, during a text-based discussion, Morgan incorporated the word "innate" taking the frame off the table to show us, while describing her sister's skill level and ability when playing sports. After this, we noticed ourselves incorporating vocabulary words into the discussion after the students used the words themselves.

Sharing the teaching and observations taking place during each lesson is a significant part of this reflective process. It involves teachers acquiring a new discourse to talk about teaching and learning, apply the knowledge they have gained from their experiences in the collaborative groups, and develop competence as literacy specialists and coaches.

5 Fostering Collaborative Learning Communities

Classroom Communities of Practice

In this chapter, I use vignettes from the collaborative groups to illustrate how communities of practice evolved and collective knowledge was shared and created during the literacy events of guided reading, partner discussions and Socratic Seminar. When I note communities of practice, I refer to research on classroom communities according to Wenger (1998), who described them as communities of practice that consist of groups of people who formally or informally develop a collection of shared knowledge, practices, resources, and ways of doing. Communities of practice cultivate a sense of belonging among individuals as they discuss common passions or concerns. They constitute social spaces in which members are given opportunities to learn from one another and in essence, they become collaborative co-learners. Valerie Kinloch (2012) reminded us that it is essential for teacher educators and teachers work alongside students to co-create opportunities for meaningful learning and understand that teaching content should consist of learning from a variety of texts and experiences generated by both teachers and students.

Within this approach, it is particularly critical to build and sustain teacher-student relationships as they are essential to the process of developing trust and supportive connections among students and teachers (Daniels & Zemelman, 2014). Throughout our preparation for the practicum, I used models and scaffolds in our conversations that involved ways for teachers to create an environment to expand their learning and construct a shared learning community with students they would work with in their collaborative inquiry groups. In order for this to happen effectively, teachers too had to have a willingness to recognize the knowledge students already had and use it to engage in co-ownership with students to provide them a space to think and collaborate.

Emergence of Inquiry-Based Learning

As evidence in this book indicates, inquiry learning is about empowering students to want to find out answers to essential questions. Harvey and Daniels published the book *Comprehension and Collaboration* (2009), in which they revel in the rebirth of inquiry-based learning in that it encourages collaboration. Wolk (2008) explained the benefits of collaborative inquiry in

> curriculum that is not just the facts and skills we teach, but the knowledge we create together and the understandings and connections that each learner makes from that knowledge. Teaching through inquiry considers our work a failure if students do not leave school filled with questions and the yearning to explore them.
>
> (p. 12)

Around the same time, Darling-Hammond et al. (2009) recommended an application of inquiry-based curriculum. She and her colleagues argued that when thinking globally, "education must help students learn how to learn in powerful ways so they can manage the demands of changing information, technologies, jobs, and social conditions" (p. 12). The authors suggest the desired framework for students to think in this manner "requires sustained student engagement, collaboration, research, management of resources, and the development of an ambitious performance or product" (p. 12). A lot to swallow and a challenge to be sure for current and future educators as well as those preparing them. So, how to best respond to this challenge? Perhaps the next section may lead us closer to the answer.

Connecting the Dots: Forming Effective Learning Environments

A major insight from Kinloch's (2012) work was the focus on teaching as a reciprocal act where students are seen as co-constructors of knowledge. She cites evidence from her study in two high school classrooms demonstrating how students and teachers engage in thoughtful dialogue and interactions that acknowledge students' voices, choices, and lived experiences. She details pedagogical strategies teachers can utilize to collaborate with students that draw on multiple texts to connect to their personal lives.

Daniels and Ahmed (2014) described another way to effectively grow a classroom community using mini-inquiries to engage students in multiple literacy practices with a range of social studies topics. They speak to the empowering nature of acknowledging and including students' voices and interests in their teaching practices. Establishing the links between inquiry and collaborative learning involves creating a learning environment and relationships built upon trust and respect that enable all members of the community an opportunity to flourish. The comments from Kris, one of the teachers in the course, support these notions,

> Establishing a bond made the learning experience more valuable for all of us. Students had to actually adapt to understand that they would be teachers, something they [youth] had not experienced before. They [students] eventually began to initiate the engagements and lead the discussions. Our group became a safe place to be comfortable and confident as a result of our relationships.

Day One: Building a Foundation

Presenting and Selecting Unit Topics

One of the essential tenets in The International Literacy Association's Adolescent Literacy Position Statement (2012) noted the development of teacher-student relationships as leading to an understanding of value and purpose for adolescent students. They go on to say that why and how instruction occurs makes a difference in their learning, something they purport adolescents deserve. The foundation of our learning communities aligns with these beliefs.

On the first day, graduate teachers meet the middle school students, and they present an overview and description of each knowledge unit via a roundtable format. The presentations last approximately ten minutes in length via a digital platform such as PowerPoint, Prezi, iMovie, and/or Glogster. The presentations are designed to be like a teaser of the topic and highlight for students an overview of the content within the unit along with example readings, questions for discussion, and artifacts such as T-Charts, vocabulary frames, etc. that will be incorporated into the various literacy events.

While they view the presentations, students take notes on a handout that lists all the inquiry unit topics (Figure 5.1).

After they view the final presentation, students are asked to numerically rank the unit topics in the order of interest to them. Some examples of the unit topics include: (1) How does the media influence

---

Inquiry Unit Ranking Sheet

Name_____

Please rank the following unit titles in the order of your favorites (use the numbers 1, 2, 3,4, 5 with 1 being your most favorite and 4 being your least favorite)

_____ Should school sports teams be coed?

_____ Should athletes be able to use the field as a platform to protest?

_____ Should we have zoos?

_____ Do technologies/social media strengthen or hinder our personal relationships?

_____ Are stop and frisk laws ethical?

Figure 5.1 Students' unit ranking sheet.

your identity and how you view yourself? (2) Should school sports teams be coed? (3) Should free speech really be free? Keeping in line with the focus on student choice, we ensure that all students receive their first or second choice. Once the students rank their choice of topics, the graduate teachers are the ones who must decide on the topic they want to teach and partner with one of their colleagues who has an interest in teaching the same unit. This becomes an empowering experience for the students as they determine the content being taught and are recognized as competent decision-makers.

Students gave positive comments when asked how they felt about taking the lead in which knowledge units were taught. I would hear comments that it was great to have the option to pick what topic to study. Another student compared it to having the choice in class to pick a partner for work. This often makes you put in more effort to your work. Still others' comments focused on the positive motivation to learn more about a topic of interest to them.

Within each group, there may be anywhere from two-four middle school students that select the same unit. Depending upon the student choices, the graduate teachers may or may not end up teaching the actual unit they created. Since they all completed the prior course to understand the foundation and structure of the units, they are able to easily adjust the content and choose materials for specific knowledge building within the unit they are teaching.

Jumping In: The Collaborative Inquiry Groups in Action

On day two, prior to any work within the knowledge units, the groups engage in team-building activities such as games designed to learn about each other. On this same day, graduate teachers model the structure and share the identity webs they previously created, then ask each student to create his/her own identity web as seen in Figure 5.2.

Figure 5.2 Sample student identity web.

Producing and sharing of these identity webs are a powerful way for the group to begin forming supportive connections and building a learning community. For students, the identity webs are a way to characterize how they view themselves and how others see them via a visual representation. For teachers, creating identity webs aides in understanding how their identity as a teacher helps them be present with students in new and innovative ways (Daniels and Ahmad, 2014). Gee (2001) has argued that through learning, one takes on new identities and new forms of participation and knowledge. Sharing their identities and lives with students is also the first step for teachers to open up a comfortable space and begin to develop a relationship with students. As noted by one of the graduate teachers, Karen,

> We made identity webs to learn where everyone was coming from and what they valued. The students were able to get to know us and we were able to get to know them.

If one were to walk into any of the designated meeting spaces at any point, one would see several seating arrangements with two graduate teachers sitting among two-four middle school students. Sitting among each other immediately diffuses the power structure to one of shared learning where teachers and students are seen as consumers and producers of knowledge working alongside each other. What to some may have seemed a bit of an unusual arrangement was actually the beginning of a well-orchestrated literate community.

As I previously noted, developing relationships was one of the key factors to the success of this program. For that reason, there was always ten-fifteen minutes at the beginning of each session devoted to informal conversation among the group members where they shared food and spoke about their personal experiences of the day. This provided another place for the students and teachers to connect. Trisha's comments reflect the significance in taking this time,

> We started every session with icebreakers to hear the stories of each group members' day and how everyone was feeling. This ensured that we established a community.

As the conversations continued it was common to hear one of the first questions asked of everyone in the group to be how was your day? This would be followed by sharing one sweet (a positive event) and one sour (a negative event) from their day. This debriefing time also served to be a rather beneficial transition time for the middle school students who were now extending their already packed day.

VIGNETTES

Scenario 1: Guided Reading and Discussion

Smagorinsky (2001) viewed engagement not only as transactions between readers and writers and texts, but to effectively engage in the literacy practices evident within a learning community requires that students fully engage with each other. What I found to be most compelling was the depth of the relationships fostered among all members of the groups. The powerful dynamic that developed not only sparked student and teacher interest in teaching and learning in the moment (Moje, 1996), but had long-term implications in that it shifted the way students and teachers viewed teaching and learning. In particular, for students who used powerful language with evidence to support their claims.

As Karen commented,

> Our students went from being passive to becoming much more outgoing via a teacher-collaborator. The more they learned the more excited they were to learn.

Teachers Kathy and Barb, and their two students, Jim, a seventh grader, and Morgan, an eighth grader worked collaboratively on an inquiry unit around the question: Should school sports be coed? All the literacy events in their unit promoted opportunities for shared discussions among graduate teachers and middle school students using a before, during, and after format.

One such discussion took place where Karen and Barb used a think aloud, annotations, and a quick write (two- to three-sentence response to a question) to model how they focused on drawing textual evidence to support literal and inferential comprehension from the text they were reading. The teachers first posed a question to the students framing it in a way that would allow the students to connect to their background knowledge and gain perspectives from each other such as: What do you believe are the benefits to boys and girls playing sports together? The students were asked to do a think pair share and form their response to the question. Using this strategy enabled the students to debrief the question with a partner in order to draw further connections.

Morgan commented on the fact that she believed it could lead to new friendships and socialization. She continued by sharing her experiences from a physical education class where some of the girls expressed a desire to participate with the boys since they made the class more fun. Jim explained that coed sports would benefit both genders because they were playing with students from a wide range of different skills. While the conversation continued, both Barb and Karen expanded upon the students' ideas as a way to synthesize the groups' ideas and evidence related to the notion of breaking stereotypes which introduced the focus of the next text they were going to read.

Karen and Barb repeated the same steps for the second reading using think aloud and annotations to model. Halfway through the reading, they paused and asked the students to share what each was going to annotate. This process continued for the remainder of the reading with both teachers and students sharing in the annotations. At the conclusion of the second reading, the teachers introduced an interactive writing summary so each group member could contribute to a visual chart to express their ideas related to both texts. With an interactive summary, a main idea question is written on the top of chart paper. These are selected by each group member. In response, each group member chooses a color and writes a sentence related to the topic sentence. Following this discussion, Barb and Karen, who wrote alongside the students, shared their writing to build off the students' ideas and points that were brought up in the group discussion.

For example, Barb shared,

> I had this idea all along that boys would be faster and stronger, so I was always intimidated to play with them.

Karen added, "I think perhaps the more common it becomes, we can break the stereotype."

She went on to explain this would be an issue addressed in their next reading.

When I first observed the group, I felt a sense that the two students were somewhat uncomfortable sharing their ideas in dialogical conversations, perhaps because they never engaged

(*Continued*)

in this type of dialogue or collaborative context before. Yet, as their comments indicate, the students undoubtedly enjoyed their shared roles as teachers and learners when the opportunities for collaborative discussions increased as did their interpretation and understanding of the texts. I could see from the expressions on their faces how proud they were to voice their opinions and how they developed more sophisticated conversations as they became confident in their ideas.

The experiences within these spaces expanded to become outlets for students to express their voices as they were afforded an array of opportunities to demonstrate, collaborate, and enhance their literacy practices, and more specifically, display the shifts in their knowledge as they moved across the literacy events. As further evidence will show, there were continuous changes taking place in adolescents' perceptions of themselves as their level of knowledge and confidence grew from reading cycle to reading cycle. They began to position themselves in the group as learners who were capable and proud to express their views in a sophisticated manner.

Scenario 2: Word Work and Vocabulary Frames

When engaging with word work, Kathy and Barb modeled a tool called vocabulary frames, shown in Figure 5.3, to focus

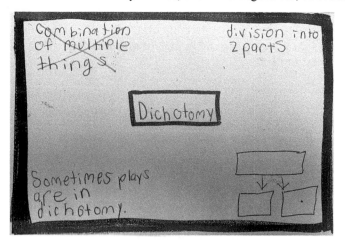

Figure 5.3 Marie's vocabulary frame.

on the comprehension and application of "foot in the door" words relevant to the readings.

Each teacher created one example of a vocabulary frame using an index card with the word noted in the middle divided into four categories: definition, antonym, sentence from the reading, and illustration. From there, the group created a vocabulary frame together and discussed the categories. Finally, the students were asked to create their own frames using an additional word from the reading. The vocabulary frames assisted the students with deeper comprehension, and they often referred to them as they engaged in the readings.

For example, in Barb's conversation about one of the words she goes into detail to explain how this using the vocabulary frames as a reference helps students expand their summaries of the overall main ideas in each reading related to whether it is appropriate to choose a boy over a girl on a sports team. It is important to note the collaboration in the group as both teachers again worked alongside the students during the introduction of the vocabulary frame and modeled how to apply the information about particular words when students encounter them in the reading.

For example, prior to reading a paragraph containing the word competence, Karen explained,

> This paragraph starts with one of our vocabulary words, competence. Let's look back at the vocabulary frame we created and review what we know about this word.

One student noted that the word meant the ability to do something successfully. Karen expanded upon this and noted how the word was applied in the text. Once again collective conversations applying knowledge of the vocabulary word assisted the group in understanding the overall message of the paragraph in the text.

Scenario 3: Employing Accountable Talk

The application of the accountable talk framework was the central foundation for our group conversations. A key premise of accountable talk is the move from teacher control to

(Continued)

student-centered conversations. There has been extensive research as to the importance of this type of classroom discourse. Fecho (2011) discussed the importance of dialogical classrooms where teachers and students engage in ongoing, reflective conversations about their reading and writing. The critical word here is ongoing, meaning that it happens over a period of time. Simply getting students to talk is not enough to sustain learning. It must be purposeful, meaning it matters what students talk about and how they talk. If we don't focus upon these two areas, talk can easily become distracting.

As Michaels, O'Connor, Hall, and Resnick (2010) asserted, "for classroom talk to promote learning it must be accountable: to the learning community, to accurate and appropriate knowledge, and to rigorous thinking" (p. 1). I noted how an evolving group dynamic developed into supportive relationships through accountable talk as students and teachers shared their ideas in the collaborative groups. I could sense the excitement of the teachers as they relinquished control and encouraged students to take on these more prominent roles as noted by one of the teachers,

> The students were more engaged because they wanted to be engaged. They initiated the engagements and eventually began to lead the discussions.

Within a different collaborative group, teaching partners Julie and Angela modeled accountable talk during guided reading of the first text in reading cycle one to help students understand the framework and show them how to select appropriate talk stem prompts in their conversations. To further enhance and support accountable talk group members used index cards and designed charts using some of the talk stems such as: Based upon my evidence, I think…, I disagree with that because…, I agree with ____ because…, I want to add to what ____ said…, (West Ed/K-12 Alliance Accountable Talk Toolkit) to guide their discussions.

There were two separate literacy events in Julie and Angela's group where accountable talk was most applicable to prompt multiple conversations were during the partner discussions and Socratic Seminar. When they engaged in partner discussions stimulating dialogue ensued as partners used their notes from readings and class discussions to articulate their claims and counterclaims of the issues presented. In the first reading cycle, Angela and Julie worked with their students to help them practice applying these talk stems as they collaborated in their partner discussions and to prepare for Socratic Seminar. As a daily observer of the partner discussions, it was fascinating for me to see the evolving group dynamic shift as the partners changed from teacher-to-teacher as they modeled the appropriate us of the talk stems in the first reading cycle, to teacher-to-student in the second reading cycle, and in reading cycle three, students worked together to initiate the conversation.

During Socratic Seminar in reading cycles one and two, Julie spoke about the way everyone in the group effectively employed the talk stems in their conversations as they discussed the pros and cons of cell phone use in school. She notes the students' language shifted during the first two debates from a more literal stance using evidence from the text toward inferential and application as they engaged in conversations that extended beyond the text. In following exchange from their Socratic debate in reading cycle three, the conversation among teachers and students continued around the essential question: What is your position on whether cell phones should be used in school?

One student responded, "Let's open that up for conversation."

Julie expanded the conversation with a prompt to find out what the students would think about the policies and cell phone use in the classroom from a teacher's perspective. "After reading about the different school policies, what would you think if teachers gave you permission to use cell phones for your projects or assignments?"

One student commented, "If it made the project more interesting, sure I would use it."

Julie replied, "Oh, so it's not necessarily the technology you're using, it would be the assignment too." The student nodded her head.

At the conclusion of the Socratic debate, Julie noted in her reflections that she thought her open-ended questions fostered a discussion between the students and enabled them

(Continued)

to critically engage in a conversation expanding their understanding about the benefits cell phones have to instructional activities.

As I observed this conversation, it became evident that accountable talk was a powerful framework that served to increase students' vocabulary and language use levels and shift the types of questions they were asking to from literal to more inference and application. Using the talk stems enabled the middle school students to build from others' ideas, think more deeply beyond the text and connect their thoughts to other perspectives. As I sat in on the group discussion, I saw a distinct shift in teachers' instructional language, prompts, and vocabulary in response to the students' language as they began to reinforce the same vocabulary from the readings used by the students to show their appreciation for students' ideas. As a result, the students began to take ownership of their own learning and became more confident expressing their knowledge of the specific texts and unit topic in general.

Julie's comments sum it up best,

> During the second cycle, my colleague and I noticed that the students were embracing the vocabulary and cell phone jargon in the articles. This changed how I spoke and what I expected of the students. Appendage was one of the vocabulary words. During each lesson I was conscious in how I used vocabulary and followed up student comments by modeling appendage and stating, "The cell phone is an appendage. That's why it probably isn't out of sight out of mind." The students continuously used the words confiscate and privilege in their discussions, and I quickly learned that they wanted to apply these words and take ownership of them. The vocabulary process started at the literal level and quickly became applicable to every lesson. The students started this trend and made me more conscious of how I needed to use vocabulary and ask questions.

The literacy events highlighted in the vignettes was a way of demonstrating how each served to support the knowledge acquisition of middle school students as well as developing teachers.

6   Expanding Connections

Reframing Literacy and Identity

In this chapter, I further examine the interplay among teacher-student relationships, identity, and literacy practices. Here, I expand upon a previous discussion regarding how the relationship among these factors should raise an awareness and addresses a somewhat outdated approach to teaching framed around assumptions about adolescents, and consequently, perpetuates myths about them. My hope is that readers of this chapter will challenge assumptions and explore a deeper understanding of adolescents taking their perspectives and lived experiences into account.

The vignettes in this chapter focus on writing events and are designed to demonstrate how the student-teacher relationships in the collaborative groups further problematize this perspective of the adolescent and serve as catalysts to explore different teaching approaches that focus upon students' expectations, needs, and desires for learning (Kinloch, 2012). That is to say, as I observed these daily negotiations among the literacy inquiry group members, I continuously noticed the shared conversations among group members to be more complex and found they provided myself and teachers in the group an important window into their lived experiences. In much the same way the social interactions among the teachers and middle school students had a significant and ongoing impact on students' perceptions of themselves as well as others in the group and were directly linked to their [adolescents] engagements with literacy. As the students adapted to understanding, they would be teachers and/or facilitators at times there were clear shifts in their perceptions of themselves.

Marcia's comment indicates evidence of this shift,

> Our students went from being passive to becoming much more
> outgoing via a teacher-collaborator. The more they learned the
> more excited they were to learn.

As further noted by her teaching partner, Kris,

> Our group became a safe place for them to be comfortable and
> confident as a result of our mutual relationships. We [teachers]
> were also learners, and they [students] were also teachers.

VIGNETTES

**Scenario 1: Post-its and T-Charts as Tools for
Collaborative Writing**

Throughout each lesson in all three reading cycles within
their knowledge unit, Barb and Karen incorporated various
genres of writing in order to support their students' literal,
inferential, and application knowledge building. When intro-
ducing a new text, they began by engaging as a group in a
quick write based upon a prompt from the teacher designed
to support the students' comprehension of the text. Implementing a quick write enabled all group members to write
about and share connections from their background knowledge and experiences to the reading. Having an opportunity
to share what they wrote prior to the reading allowed each
group member to build upon their inferential knowledge by
listening to different perspectives.

Within the reading and text-based discussion, these perspectives were further applied and referenced to support the
comprehension of subsequent texts. Throughout the readings, each group member used specific symbols located on
a chart to annotate texts. At other times they could be seen
jotting down notes within the margins, such as a connection
made to the text or the definition of a word. These annotations supported their discussions throughout the readings,
as well as when locating evidence for T-Charts, the students'
writing piece, and Socratic seminars.

The following excerpt demonstrates collaborative writing done by the group as they began to tease out the important ideas from the first two texts in reading cycle one. Before reading the texts, the students crafted a response to an open-ended quick write prompt asking: What are your feelings on boys and girls playing sports together? The goal was to get students to access their background knowledge and start thinking about their own opinions before being influenced by the text.

Both Barb and Karen wrote alongside students and after everyone was finished writing individually, each shared their response with the group.

Jim noted,

> I think boys and girls can play sports together. I was on a coed little league team and we all got along.

This shared experience sparked a discussion and brought a new perspective to the group.

Barb responded,

> Do you see more coed teams at younger ages? Do they separate boys and girls once they reach a certain age?

Morgan shared that she was also on coed recreational teams when she was younger, but now that they are in middle school teams are typically separated by gender. Students also responded to the prompt: What do you think are the benefits to boys and girls playing on the same team?

Morgan responded saying,

> I think it could lead to friendships and socialization, but there are times when my gym teacher says let's play with the boys and some of the girls groan, although some do smile....

Her response naturally led Barb, and Karen to inquire further about the experience students had in their physical education classes. The students shared what they noticed about

(Continued)

boys and girls in gym class, and mentioned factors such as the coach, the sport, and the time of day inform how boys and girls specifically act in gym class. This opened up the opportunity for further collaborative interchange as Karen and Barb shared their own memories from physical education class. Karen discussed her competitive spirit and wanting to play alongside boys, while Barb shared that playing alongside the boys made her uncomfortable in gym class. All of this discussion brought multiple perspectives to the table and served as a foundation for future guided reading as all of these issues were mentioned in various places in each of the unit texts.

In preparation for the Socratic Seminar within each reading cycle, the group created a T-Chart seen in Figure 6.1 based upon the evidence they found in each of two texts and that addressed the questions they had previously discussed in the quick write responses. Each group member used a different color marker to write their piece of evidence from text 1 on the right side and from text 2 on the left side. This method was used in the next two reading cycles as well.

The second T-Chart seen in Figure 6.2 was created as a reference for the group to use in the final Socratic Seminar. This was another collaborative project with each group member reviewing notes from all of their texts in the unit. The focused task for this chart was on pulling specific evidence from each text that would be supportive in defending claims (advantages) and counterclaims (disadvantages) that addressed the essential question of the unit: Should school sports be coed? Each group member found evidence they deemed important within each reading and wrote it on individual post-it notes along with the number of the text as a reference. Within this writing, each group member paraphrased specific evidence within the text, as there was not enough room on the post-it to write the entire sentence. Each added their post-it notes to the particular item listed on each column of the T-Chart.

The writing crafted within each these T-Charts was supportive for both Morgan and Jim when creating their draft

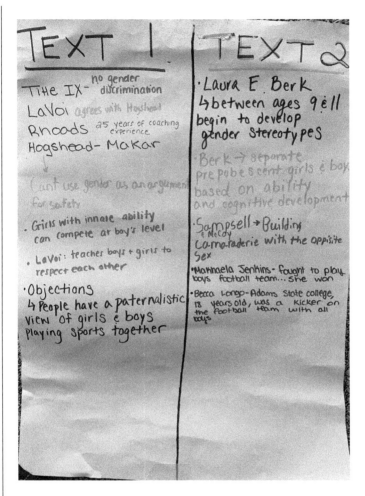

Figure 6.1 T-Chart two-column notes connecting text-evidence.

and final argumentative writing pieces. In drafting their writing pieces, both students utilized the multiple readings, discussions, and tools such as the T-Charts from all three reading cycles to summarize their thoughts and design an overall plan for writing their final argumentative piece.

(Continued)

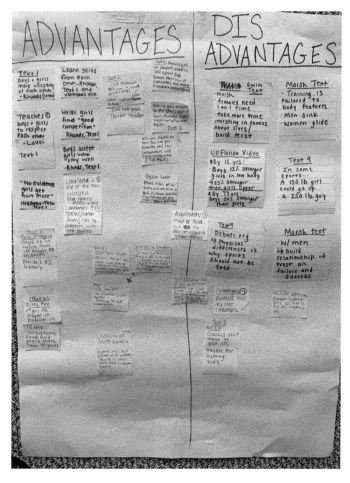

Figure 6.2 T-Chart post-it notes categorizing advantages and disadvantages.

Scenario 2: Expanding Text Connections

Some of the most effective, collective knowledge building occurred when students had the opportunity to write about and discuss several texts as a group that delved into the pros and cons of cell phone use in class. For example, in reading cycle one, the students first completed their responses to a four-square organizer, and then referred to it their conversation regarding the first two readings. The students discussed the following prompts from the organizer: (1) Do you think teaching cell phone etiquette will have any effect on cell phone use in class? Why or why not? (2) Are cell phones really "out of sight out of mind"? Why or why not? (3) How can cell phones be used as a tool to enhance learning? (4) What impact would banishing cell phones have on schools?

While discussing, one student said,

> I don't think cell phones are 'out of sight out of mind'. Students still think about what they might be missing or who might be texting them.

Another student referenced a talk stem and replied,

> I agree. If a phone is in a student's pocket, that person might feel it buzzing and it could be a distraction to learning.

Based upon the multiple conversations, I observed that day, evidence of collective knowledge was continuously building because there were ongoing opportunities for everyone to share their notes and listen to different perspectives to understand each other's point of view and apply the knowledge to their own experiences. These aided each group member the tools to frame their decision on the issue as to whether cell phones were a pro or con in the classroom.

After reading several texts, discussing and writing about cell phone use in a variety of other school contexts, Angela, Julie, and their students made the decision to apply the knowledge they learned about the pros and cons of cell phones and co-create a hypothetical cell phone policy. Although everyone in the group participated, this activity was primarily led by the students who determined what policies they felt were important to include.

The final written piece contained four categories. The first was instructional (uses permitted within the classroom setting), non-instructional (locations in the school other than the classroom such as hallways, cafeteria, etc., where cell phone use might be permitted), consequences/violations, and what students should do in the event they need to use a cell phone to contact a family member in an emergency.

(*Continued*)

Students employed talk stems when discussing where cell phones should and shouldn't be allowed in their hypothetical school. One student noted,

> I think we need to include that cell phones can be used in non-instructional areas such as the cafeteria, hallways, and on the busses.

Another student responded to that saying,

> I agree with all of those places that you mentioned, but I also think we should include that students can use cell phones during study hall as long as they get it approved by the teacher and they are using it for educational purposes.

At this point students were not referring directly to the accountable talk stem examples; rather, as this conversation demonstrates, students were already applying them naturally in their conversations. Students were also displaying interpretative and application knowledge throughout this activity agreeing and disagreeing as to what specific information should or should not be included in the policy document and employ language that would effectively convey their ideas.

Drafting the Written Argument

At the end of the third reading cycle, the groups engage in writing workshop where students gather all of their writing pieces from the unit such as quick writes, notes from partner discussions and seminars, along with the numerous tools used for writing such as post-its, T-Charts, annotations, etc. The students use these to organize their final written argument based upon their stance to the essential question. During this time, they tap all the resources listed above while they work collaboratively if needed to confer with other group members to frame their argument, compile evidence to support their claims, and complete a written argumentative piece. The students have the option to decide whether their piece will be handwritten or completed and printed as a word document. The final products are shared in a format such as a read aloud, poster display, etc. as part of the students' presentation on the final celebration night.

Multiliteracies

The multiliteracies framework was significant to the design of the culminating project in that it informs our ways of knowing how adolescents interact and construct meaning within their worlds. The term multiliteracies was coined by a group of scholars known as the New London Group (1996). They met to discuss the increase in linguistic and cultural diversity, and to elaborate on the multiplicity of text forms that were emerging within the digital and economic scenes as a result of globalization. Luke and Elkins (2002) coined this, *new times.*

Multiliteracy theory is concerned with the "what" of literacy in new times, that is, what people need to know, as well as the "how" of gaining the needed tools to be functional, productive, and successful in the new digital and global market (New London Group, 1996).

Central to this perspective is context. The literacies that are valued and used in different contexts depend upon what is valued in and by the community of users, similar to our collaborative communities. Multiliteracies represent the identities and practices that are relevant to the context of this course in that throughout the knowledge units, middle school students constantly negotiated the constructions of their literate practices and reconstructed those practices to meet their literate needs. This framework informed our decision to offer students the opportunity to express their argument in a digital platform such as those described in the next section.

Engaging with Multimodal Literacies

As a secondary educator, I would be remiss if I did not acknowledge the ever-present role of digital media in the life of adolescents today. In their position statement on adolescent literacy, The International Literacy Association (2012) vehemently supported this notion with a call to action to all those working with adolescents:

Specifically, instruction is needed that will enable students to comprehend and construct a range of multimodal texts across genres, disciplines, and digital spaces. Teaching comprehension and composition, while always a mainstay of the school curriculum, is even more crucial today. Likewise, the stakes have never seemed higher for teaching students to think critically about what they see, hear, view, and construct in the relatively untamed world of Web 2.0.

(p. 8)

When designing this course and the final product, it was essential to not restrict students' use of print literacy; rather, my desire was to provide them with opportunities to express their ideas within a broader view of literacy. For the second part of their presentation, students were given the choice of several digital platforms to create an interactive, multimodal version of their final argument. Some of the options include PowerPoint, Prezi, iMovie, and Glogster platforms. It should be noted that these were also selected due to their ease of access within the school's digital network.

For this project, each student expanded the info from the single written mode and paired them with other multiple modes of communication that included images, video clips, and songs, to further convey their argument in a more interactive manner. In preparing for the celebration night, students create talking points on index cards to supplement their visual presentations on individual laptops.

Concluding Thoughts

The ongoing, daily interactions within these learning communities played such a significant role in mediating multiple modes of being a reader and writer for the middle school participants. In these dialogical discussions among the collaborative inquiry group, middle school students drew upon multiple texts and tools to express their opinions, emotions, and connect to their personal literate lives. Teacher-student relationships, collaborative literacy practices, instructional strategies and activities within the learning communities weaved together to become integral components to the overall success and collective knowledge building.

Throughout the semester I noticed first-hand the influence of quality relationships on the changing/evolving roles of teachers and students within the collaborative groups. I witnessed the continuous shifts in the level of knowledge for both teachers and students as they progressed through each reading cycle in the knowledge units. Opportunities for teachers to engage in collaborative teaching opens them to experience the unique and personal academic literacy histories adolescents possess that influence who they choose to develop relationships with, how they value literacy, and shape how they view their work. Thus, there remains an ongoing need to continue to raise awareness regarding the many impacts of identity on adolescents' learning and their sense of belonging. It is becoming more obvious that we cannot draw a separation between the content being taught and the social and emotional concerns of adolescent students. By exploring the ways collaborative learning can serve to shape and reshape identity and disciplinary literacy practices, secondary teachers can build upon them by tapping the myriad of experiences students have to make sense of the new knowledge they learn and continue to learn. My hope is that by listening more intently to their voices, our theories about adolescents can continue to be contested, and we as educators will be compelled to revise and expand what we think we know about them.

7 Celebrating Our Literacy Learning

Tapping Funds of Knowledge

The scenarios in Chapters 5 and 6 highlighted how participation in the collaborative groups fostered respectful partnerships and reciprocal relationships among teachers and students. In this chapter, I extend these ideas to include another essential component of the course, connections with families and communities. Within the course, there is the expectation that teachers interact and engage with families and the community in ways that respect the diversity of the lived experiences represented by the members. As the title of this section indicates, it was vital to the success of the collaboration for teachers to recognize and draw upon the funds of knowledge (Moll, Amanti, Neff, & Gonzales, 1992) their students brought from families and the community and use these resources in their teaching. Within the collaborative groups, tapping these valuable sociocultural practices alongside content was an effective way to build off each other's literacies, yet also learn together.

Family Engagement

Although we are only present at the school for a semester, over that time we do become part of the school community. Much of this is through the weekly connections with families via conversations and written communications. These conversations occur on a bi-weekly basis, often with a family member who comes to pick up the student at the end of the session. Teachers are also expected to communicate in writing via a few course assignments. At the end of the first week of class, teachers create a written letter that welcomes families of each of their students and thanks them for the opportunity to work with their child. Teachers introduce themselves and provide an overview of the essential question and related content of the knowledge unit.

At the end of each subsequent week, teachers create a written letter given to families that highlights literacy events, readings, strategies, tools, etc. that the group employed during that particular reading cycle. The second half of the letter includes a section on student learnings and celebrates the markers of student successes in their collaborative roles in the inquiry group.

At the conclusion of the course, teachers write an extended letter as seen in the excerpts from a letter written by Angela, Julie, thanking the family of one of their students for providing the opportunity to work with him. The content of the letter is individualized for each student weaving positive aspects of his insights and contributions within the group via relationships and interactions. It further addresses the markers of student engagement such as shifts in knowledge levels, and participation noted across the semester related to language and vocabulary, comprehension, writing, and interactions related to the various roles in the group. They also discuss some of the instructional supports such as visuals, annotations, etc. that enhanced students' understandings. These are important to discuss since they may be effective extensions to learning for students to use at home or in other school contexts. Family communication also occurs in person on our celebration night that will be discussed in the next section.

The excerpt from their letter speaks to the authenticity of the relationships established in the group and how these experiences were contributing factors that shaped and were shaped by the student's identity and literacy practices:

Dear Family of _____,

It has been an absolute pleasure to get to know and work with **student**. Each session he inspired his peers to critically analyze texts, use text evidence to support his thinking, and ask questions. He used accountable talk stems in discussions to honor his peer's thoughts and opinions before adding his own information. As the semester gained momentum, his personality began to shine. His enthusiasm sparked interesting conversations and pushed his group members to think outside the box. He was taking notes independently and applying the talk stems regularly in the conversations. During the last month, he flourished. Not only has he continued to take a lead role in conversations, he has shared that leadership role with his peers. He knows when to sit back, listen, and let another group member take the reign. He inquisitively listens to his peers' input, and they know he will ask clarifying questions before adding his own ideas.

This letter excerpt speaks to the teachers' thinking about the nature of the group interactions and their implications to their teaching and the student's learning.

Family Celebration Night

At the end of the semester, the teachers and students in the collaborative inquiry groups invite families to a celebration to share their accomplishments. This is truly an opportunity for students to be recognized as co-creators and producers of knowledge as they take on the primary roles and present their culminating projects, both written and digital to their family, friends, and the school community. It also provides an authentic purpose and audience for the presentations.

Each student sits at his or her own table. On the front of each table is a sign inscribed with the student's name and the title of the presentation. Teachers in each group sit alongside as facilitators who enthusiastically support their students. As a starting point the audience informally gathers around a specific student's table as each student highlights various tools and writing he or she created in the collaborative groups. Each highlights their written argument piece followed by a presentation of the argument via a digital platform.

For teachers, engaging with families on celebration night provides another occasion to raise their level of comfort communicating with students and their families. The large turnout of parents, families, friends, teachers, and administrators further solidifies the success and ongoing support of our program. At the conclusion of the presentations, everyone partakes in refreshments, sitting together and conversing as they learn more about each other.

The comments from my interview with Marie, a student participant sums up the reasons why she returned for a second year.

JOLENE: What made you want to return to the groups for a second year?

MARIE: I like that at the end there is a big celebration where show our work. I am also better in all my other classes for the rest of the year because of the group projects and other skills I learn in the class. It makes doing the work more fun because the teachers have our group try out all different things. Like they are grad students, so they are learning new things and teaching with us, so I get to find out some ways to learn that I like better.

JOLENE: How do you like working with the teachers in your group?

MARIE: I think it is cool. Like in school we do things in the beginning of the year everyone says one fact about each other and the teacher, and that's how it is for the rest of the year. Here, we do so many activities to get to know each other and it's just more fun.

JOLENE: How do you think that effects your learning?

MARIE: It's fun to learn because I like being able to use articles as a group to highlight and get to talk about what we are reading. I don't do that in class because we have books.

At the family celebration, Marie's mother told me how much her daughter benefitted from her experiences in the class. She saw noticeable changes in Marie's work in school and overall in her competence and confidence as a learner.

The Value of Collaborative Partnerships

As I noted in the beginning, I believe one of the audiences for this book to be those who are practicing teachers in the secondary schools. To that end, it essential to hear how collaborative partnerships directly impact those who work in the schools. The following comments are from Sherry Guice, the reading specialist with whom I have collaborated for the past couple years. She speaks to the value of building partnerships and forming relationships and the resulting successes of those continued partnerships:

> School-university collaborations are important to me for several reasons. First, I strongly believe that we need excellent teachers, and I worry that we have far too few young adults entering our profession. For those of us dedicated to teaching and improving the lives of children, we can potentially have an influence on the future of our schools and teachers by working together in collaborative school-based learning environments. I feel that it is my responsibility as a member of our education community and school community that I strive to play some role in bettering the state of teaching by working to open our school to the university.
>
> Collaboration has the potential to illustrate the power that teaching can have on one's life as a professional. After thirty-five years of teaching, I still find it exciting and rewarding, yet at times, difficult. It is my hope that the graduate students see

research into practice in my classroom, the books, the anchor charts and other artifacts of my work as a reading specialist embodies. I serve as a live demonstration of my own continual learning so they too may embrace the notion that one strives to be an excellent teacher through reading, studying, modeling, reflection, modifying, etc... My goal and motivation are to foster the idea of teaching as a lifelong learning experiences with grand payoffs in the form of growth and relationships with students.

It is important that the students in our school be exposed to these partnerships so that college does not seem remote, but rather, more accessible to them. The interactions and relationships that our middle school students have with professors and graduate students can not only help them grow as confident thinkers and learners, but also expose them to new ideas and a voice that may not have been fostered in our instruction.

Future Directions and Questions

Implications for Practice

My hope is that this book will continue to inform the practice of those who work as secondary teachers and teacher educators. I believe it is of utmost importance to those who work in these contexts continue to consider how literacy has changed, is being redefined and how adolescents use literacies in different ways. As Luke and Elkins (2000) concluded:

> We must address the complex issues around adolescents' access to and alienation from social institutions; their positions and identities within cultural fields of community life and work, education, and consumption.
>
> (p. 1)

By observing how successful teacher-student relationships create and/or sustain literacies, we can continue to glean insights into how classroom practices and communities may further embolden these relationships to address other aspects of literacy in the various disciplines.

The course model presented in this book, particularly with regard to the seminar, can serve to inform a different lens to take up professional development that moves away from the more typical day or two professional development currently in place in schools. As noted by Bean (2015), if we do not provide strategies that are anchored to educators' beliefs about learning, they cannot be sustained.

In this course model, seminars served an important function in that they provided the graduate teachers opportunities to reflect on their own practice, yet at the same time collaborate with their colleagues as literacy coaches. Both experiences serve as catalysts for change to motivate teachers in their beliefs about their own learning and that of their students.

Implications for Future Research

I believe some aspects of this course could be explored for future research in the area of practitioner or teacher research. Bogdan and Biklen (2003) described the benefits of employing teacher research, "the approach requires that educators be more rigorous and observant in collecting information in order to recognize their own points of view and to break through the stereotypical images that may govern their behavior toward others" (p. 230). In both the practicum and seminar, graduate teachers were provided multiple opportunities to examine the way students learn. Having these experiences afforded them the necessary time to further transform their beliefs about teaching and learning.

Employing teacher research can be an opportunity for teachers to examine the way adolescents' social interactions and relationships serve to shape and reshape their literacy and to use this knowledge to assist students with literacy across the disciplines. The result may very well be an increase in the number of students who want to do well in their disciplinary literacy practices.

A final area for further exploration given the global context in which we live might be research into the use of virtual learning communities. Although I have not employed virtual learning communities in this course, it is an area I do want to consider as I think about the future contexts and opportunities for online learning.

Remembering Why Relationships Matter

The inquiry groups empowered teachers and students to work collaboratively toward a common goal, learning. The context of this course served as a bridge connecting members of the school community, families, and the university in ways that were perhaps transformative to all. Hopefully, this partnership will continue to expand possibilities for future collaborations.

I leave the reader with the following comments from Barb and Melanie, two graduate teachers who vividly recount how their participation in the collaborative inquiry groups turned out to be much more than just a required practicum teaching experience.

In the first paragraph of her final assignment, Barb wrote,

> During the past several weeks, I have had the pleasure of working collaboratively with Morgan and Jim. At the start of this program, both admitted that they do not typically enjoy reading. However, throughout our time together it became clear that they are both fluent readers and strong writers. I observed Morgan as she read an entire verse novel by Sonya Sones prior to some of our last sessions. When she finished this book, she was overwhelmed with emotion and stated, "I don't usually like reading, so I am having a moment." From my conversations with her, I learned that Morgan enjoys this author and has read several of her other books. Jim is involved in drama club and plays the trumpet. Although he may not always enjoy reading books, he reads music, scripts, and memorizes lines. Although it took a little time for both Morgan and Jim to warm up to the collaborative arrangement in our group, they eventually became animated and active participants.

Melanie's words echo a similar theme,

> I would absolutely say that our relationship impacted the students' level of engagement in the literacy instruction. As in any instructional setting, when students feel comfortable and part of a learning community where they are mutually respected and heard, they are more willing to take chances, state their questions and concerns, and express their feelings. By the end of our time together, the typical "teacher" role was almost non-existent...we were a group of four all working and learning together.

References

Alvermann, D. (2001). *Effective literacy instruction.* Executive summary and paper Commissioned by the National Reading Conference. Chicago, IL: National Reading Conference.

Alvermann, D. (2009). Social constructions of adolescence and young people's literacies. In L. Christenbury, R. Bomer, & P. Smagorinsky (Eds.), *Handbook of adolescent literacy research* (pp. 14–28). New York: Guilford Press.

Bean, R. (2015). The role of reading specialists and literacy coaches in schools, classrooms, and communities. In R. Bean (Ed.), *The reading specialist: Leadership and coaching for the classroom, school, and community* (3rd ed., pp. 1–19). New York: Guilford Press.

Biancarosa, G., & Snow, K. (2004). *Reading next—A vision for action and research in middle and high school literacy.* New York: Carnegie Corporation of New York.

Bogdan, R. & Biklen, S. (2003). *Qualitative research for education: An introduction to theory and methods.* Boston, MA: Allyn and Bacon.

Brozo, W. (2017). Adolescent literacies and identities inside and outside of school. In W. Brozo (Ed.), *Disciplinary and content literacy for today's adolescents: Honoring diversity and building competence* (6th ed., pp. 1–28). New York: Gilford Press.

Daniels, H., & Ahmed, S. (2014). *Upstanders: How to engage middle school hearts and minds with inquiry.* Portsmouth, NH: Heinemann.

Daniels, H., & Zemelman, S. (2014). *Subjects matter: Exceeding standards through powerful content-area reading* (2nd ed.). Portsmouth, NH: Heinemann.

Darling-Hammond, L., et al. (2008). *Powerful learning: What we know about teaching for understanding.* San Francisco, CA: Jossey-Bass.

Dillon, D.R., Moje, E.B., & O'Brien, D.G. (2000). Reexamining the roles of learner, text, and context in secondary literacy. *Journal of Educational Research, 93,* 165–180.

Elish-Piper, L., L'Allier, S.K., Manderino, M., & Di Domenico, P. (2016). *Collaborative coaching for disciplinary literacy.* New York: Guilford Press.

Fecho, B. (2011). *Writing in the dialogical classroom: Students and teachers responding to the texts of their lives.* Urbana, IL: National Council of Teachers of English.

Ferguson, A.A. (2002). *Bad boys: Public schools in the making of masculinity.* Ann Arbor, MI: University of Michigan Press.

Finders, M.J. (1998/1999). Raging hormones: Stories of adolescence and implications for teacher preparation. *Journal of Adolescent and Adult Literacy, 42,* 252–263.

Gallimore, R., & Tharp, R. (1990). Teaching mind in society: Teaching schooling and literate discourse. In L. Moll (Ed.), *Vygotsky and education: Instructional implications and applications of socio-historical psychology* (pp. 101–110). New York: Cambridge University Press.

Gee, J. (1996). *Social linguistics and literacy: Ideology in discourses* (2nd ed.). London: Falmer Press.

Gee, J. (2001). Reading as situated language: A sociocultural perspective. *Journal of Adolescent and Adult Literacy, 44,* 714–725.

Graham, S., & Perin, D. (2007). *Writing next—Effective strategies to improve writing of adolescents in middle and high schools.* New York: Carnegie Corporation of New York.

Guthrie, J., Klauda, S., & Ho, A. (2013). Modeling the relationships among reading instruction, motivation, engagement, and achievement for adolescents. *Reading Research Quarterly, 48,* 9–26.

Hall, S. (1996). Introduction: Who needs identity? In S. Hall & P. du Gay (Eds.), *Questions of cultural identity* (pp. 1–17). London: SAGE.

Harvey, S., & Daniels, H. (2009). *Comprehension and collaboration: Inquiry circles in action.* Portsmouth, NH: Heinemann.

Heath, S.B. (1983). *Ways with words: Language, life and work in communities and classrooms.* Cambridge, MA: Cambridge University Press.

Hull, G., & Schultz, K. (2001). Literacy and learning out of school: A review of theory and research. *Review of Educational Research, 71,* 575–611.

International Reading Association. (2012). *Adolescent literacy* [Position statement]. Newark, DE: International Reading Association.

Kinloch, V. (2012). *Crossing boundaries: Teaching and learning with urban youth.* New York: Teachers College Press.

Lambert, L. (1998). How to build leadership capacity. *Education Week, 55*(7), 17–19.

Lee, V., Smith, J., Perry, T., & Smylie, M. (1999). *Social support, academic press, and student achievement: A view from the middle grades in Chicago.* Chicago, IL: Consortium on Chicago School Research.

Luke, A., & Elkins, J. (2000). Re/mediating adolescent literacies. *Journal of Adolescent and Adult Literacy, 43,* 396–399.

Luke, A., & Elkins, J. (2002). Towards a critical, worldly literacy. *Journal of Adolescent and Adult Literacy, 45,* 668–673.

McCarthy, S. (2001). Identity construction in elementary readers and writers. *Reading Research Quarterly, 36,* 122–151.

Michaels, S., O'Connor, C., Hall, M., & Resnick, L.B. (2010). *Accountable talk sourcebook: For classroom conversation that works.* Pittsburgh, PA: University of Pittsburgh.

Moje, E. (1996). I teach students, not subjects: Understanding teacher-student relationships as contexts for literacy practices in a high school content classroom. *Reading Research Quarterly, 31,* 172–195.

Moje, E. (2002). Re-framing adolescent literacy research for new times: Studying youth as a resource. *Reading Research and Instruction, 41,* 211–228.

Mok, J. (2008). Distributed cognition in learning. *The International Journal of Learning, 15* (4), 151–159.

Moll, L., Amanti, C., Neff, D., & Gonzales, N. (1992). Funds of knowledge for teaching: Using a qualitative approach to connect homes and classrooms. *Theory into Practice, 21* (2), 132–141.

New London Group. (1996). A pedagogy of multiliteracies: Designing social futures. *Harvard Educational Review, 66* (1), 60–91.

Noddings, N. (2005). *The challenge to care in schools: An alternative approach to education* (2nd ed.). New York: Teachers College Press.

O'Brien, D.G. (1998). Multiple literacies in a high school program for "at-risk" adolescents. In D.E. Alvermann, K.A. Hinchman, D.W. Moore, S.F. Phelps, & D.R. Waff (Eds.), *Reconceptualizing the literacies in adolescents' lives* (pp. 27–49). Mahwah, NJ: Erlbaum.

O'Brien, D.G. (2006). "Struggling adolescents' engagement in multimediating: Countering the institutional construction of competence. In D.E. Alvermann, K.A. Hinchman, D.W. Moore, S.F. Phelps, & D.R. Waff (Eds.), *Reconceptualizing the literacies in adolescents' lives* (2nd Ed., pp. 29–46). Mahwah, NJ: Erlbaum.

Roth, W. (1997). Graphing: Cognitive ability or practice? *Science Education, 81* (1), 91–106.

Santa, C. (2006). A vision for adolescent literacy: Ours or theirs? *Journal of Adolescent and Adult Literacy, 49,* 466–478.

Serafini, F. (2001). *The reading workshop: Creating space for readers.* Portsmouth, NH: Heinemann.

Sfard, A., & Prusak, A. (2005). Telling identities: In search of an analytic tool for investigating learning as a culturally shaped activity. *Educational Researcher, 34,* 14–22.

Shanahan, T., & Shanahan, C. (2008). Teaching disciplinary literacy to adolescents: Rethinking content-area literacy. *Harvard Educational Review, 78* (1), 40–59.

Sheehy, M., & Malavasic, J. T. (2014). *How are we doing? A case study exploring a two-course sequence in academic argument and knowledge building for secondary literacy specialists implementing common core standards.* Roundtable presented at the Literacy Research Association Conference, Marco Island, Florida.

Smagorinsky, P. (2001). If meaning is constructed, what is it made from? Toward a cultural theory of reading. *Review of Educational Research, 71,* 133–169.

Sutherland, L.M. (2005). Black adolescent girls' use of literacy practices to negotiate boundaries of ascribed identity. *Journal of Literacy Research, 37,* 365–406.

Toll, C. (2005). *The literacy coach's survival guide: Essential questions and practical answers.* Newark, DE: International Reading Association.

Toll, C. (2014). *The literacy coach's survival guide: Essential questions and practical answers* (2nd ed.). Newark, DE: International Reading Association.

Vadeboncoeur, J.D., & Stevens, L.P. (Eds.). (2005). *Re/constructing "the adolescent".* New York: Peter Lang.

Wells, M.C. (1996). *Literacies lost: When students move from progressive middle school to a traditional high school.* New York: Teachers Press.

Wenger, E. (1998). *Communities of practice: Learning, meaning, and identity.* Cambridge, UK: Cambridge University Press.

West Ed/K-12 Alliance: *Accountable talk toolkit.* Retrieved from: http://www.ces.rcs.k12.tn.us/web_uploads: Accessed October 2018.

Wolk, S. (2003). Hearts and minds. *Educational Leadership, 61* (1), 14–18.

Wolk, S. (2008). School as inquiry. *Phi Delta Kappan, 90,* 115–122.

Zhang, J., & Sun, Y. (2011). Reading for idea advancement in a grade 4 knowledge building community. *Instructional Science, 39* (4), 429–452.

Index

Note: *Italic* page numbers refer to figures.